A Dog in a Million

ᴴ ᴀᴢᴇʟ Cᴀʀᴛᴇʀ has spent her life around animals. At the
ᵃᵍᵉ of four she recalls putting a lead on her cat in an
ᵃᵗᵗᵉ mpt to take it for a walk in the woods next to her
ⁱᵈʸˡˡ ic family home in deepest rural Sussex. Realising that
ᶜᵃᵗˢ were not as accommodating as dogs, she switched her
al legiance and a life working with animals and training
do gs began.

Bᴏɴɴɪᴇ was a finalist in the Kennel Club 'Friends for
Liᶠᵉ' competition at Crufts in 2008 and has appeared on
teˡev ision and in the press in the UK, USA and Europe.

A Dog in a Million

Hazel Carter

preface
publishing

Published by Preface 2009

10 9 8 7 6 5 4 3 2 1

First published in Great Britain in 2009 by Preface Publishing
1 Queen Anne's Gate
London SW1H 9BT

An imprint of The Random House Group

www.rbooks.co.uk
www.prefacepublishing.co.uk

Addresses for companies within The Random House Group Limited
can be found at www.randomhouse.co.uk

The Random House Group Limited Reg. No. 954009

A CIP catalogue record for this book is available from the British Library

ISBN 978 1 84809 104 7

The Random House Group Limited supports The Forest Stewardship
Council (FSC), the leading international forest certification organisation.
All our titles that are printed on Greenpeace-approved FSC-certified paper
carry the FSC logo. Our paper procurement policy can be found at
www.rbooks.co.uk/environment

Mixed Sources
Product group from well-managed
forests and other controlled sources
www.fsc.org Cert no. TT-COC-2139
© 1996 Forest Stewardship Council

Typeset in Sabon by Palimpsest Book Production Limited,
Grangemouth, Stirlingshire

Printed and bound in Great Britain by
CPI Bookmarque, Croydon CR0 4TD

To Fred with all my love

'Near this spot are deposited the remains of one who possessed Beauty without Vanity, Strength without Insolence, Courage without Ferocity, and all the Virtues of Man, without his Vices. This Praise, which would be unmeaning Flattery if inscribed over human ashes, is but a just tribute to the Memory of Boatswain, a Dog.'

George Gordon, Lord Byron. The epitaph inscribed on the gravestone of his beloved Newfoundland.

Contents

Acknowledgements

Many thanks to Karen Dolby and all at Preface Publishing for their hard work.

I would like to thank my friend Jo who kindly gave up her time to walk Connie when I could not manage it; a very special bond developed between them which they still have today. Many thanks also to Sas, another friend who has regularly brought her black Labrador, Oliver, to play with Connie. He is still her best friend. My sister-in-law Stella has been a wonderful help and so was her Welsh Springer Spaniel Trampus, the most perfect gentleman of a dog who taught Connie how to behave and play gently with an elderly dog.

How can I possibly thank Connie for everything she has given me? From the very first day I brought her home she has always been sweet, gentle, loving and loyal. With her intelligence and willingness she has been a joy to train. When the going was very rough it would have been easy to sink into deep depression and apathy, but how could I let this happen when I looked into her bright eyes as she waited expectantly for the next game. As I am writing this she is, as usual, curled up beside me. Thank you Connie, if it were not for you there would be no book.

Lastly, but most importantly, I want to thank my wonderful husband Fred for all his help, support and love over the years and on this new venture.

1

A New Puppy

'I just know this could be the perfect dog for you,' Anne had reasoned. 'I've known the breeder for years. You'll like her and she'll like you. Besides, what harm is there in looking? You're not committing yourself to anything . . .'

Anne was an old friend and the breeder of my beloved Newfoundland, Christie, who had died almost two years before. And so a few days later, I drove up to the small holding in Derbyshire with my eldest son, Barry, just to take a look.

I had grown up and spent my whole life with dogs and I missed my last one terribly. Walks just weren't the same without a canine companion and I found myself missing Christie's eager greeting when I arrived home. I had waited two years following two hip replacements to decide whether I wanted to take on another large Newfoundland. But once you love a breed they become part of your life. Now I realised I had to have another Newfoundland.

It was early November 2005, a perfect crisp day with a clear blue sky and the leaves still clinging to the trees in myriad autumnal shades, deepest umber to gleaming gold. We drew up outside the old farmhouse and as I got out of the car I saw a puppy rounding the corner of the building. She trotted along the path towards me looking like a very important little person, curious and confident, tail wagging happily. She was a sturdy, compact, well-rounded Newfoundland puppy, very black and fluffy. She pushed her velvet muzzle into my hand as I knelt to greet her and, stroking her soft fur in response, I was instantly smitten.

She gazed up at me with small friendly brown eyes and something about her face reminded me of a baby bear. She was a comical little thing, but a thoughtful one too. When I spoke gently to her she carefully tilted her head to one side, listening intently to every word. There was no question about it: she was the dog for me. Her breeder asked me lots of questions to make sure I was absolutely the right person for her precious puppy but all was quickly settled. She had originally been destined for a new home in Ireland, but luckily for me there had been a last-minute problem. We agreed I would return in one week to collect her.

All the way home in the car we discussed names for her. Nothing seemed quite right until Barry suggested 'Connie'. Most of my dogs' names have begun with the letter 'C' but nothing we could think of seemed to fit until my son came up with this. It sounded just right, a rather old-fashioned, prim and proper name that suited her personality perfectly.

A week later, my husband Fred and I arrived back in Derbyshire to collect Connie. At ten weeks old, she was the last of her litter to leave. While the paperwork was being completed I was able to study her more closely. She was busily exploring the sitting room which was completely unfamiliar to her. She was a rather funny looking puppy with her tail held straight up in the air and an appealingly cute but rather ugly little face, her character friendly and open, neither too timid nor too bold. Already she was showing signs of her great intelligence by carefully pulling a book from the shelves which she studied curiously – it was about dog training!

The back of our Volvo estate had been prepared for the new puppy, with a cardboard box bed surrounded by puppy-training paper in case of emergency. It was a long trip back to our home in Sussex and as she had not yet had her injections there was no question of stopping en route. As we were about to set off, I looked down at the puppy snuggled in my arms and decided she would be happier with me on the back seat, to reassure and comfort her on her very first ride in a car. Sure enough, she cuddled close to me and slept for almost the whole journey.

Absent-mindedly stroking her soft, matt-black fur, I had plenty of time to daydream. I always find car journeys a perfect opportunity to let my mind wander. Now I began to think about all that I planned to do with Connie. There have always been animals in my life, and since I was a small girl I have been interested in dog training. Over the years this developed into a one-to-one counselling service, advising owners on behavioural problems in their dogs long before the term 'behaviourist' was even invented.

Christie, my last Newfoundland, had been a wonderful companion. I had taken her training further than I had ever tried to do before, prompted primarily by my own state of health. I had congenital hip problems and was becoming increasingly immobile, so that even simple tasks like picking up a pen that I'd dropped, getting up out of an armchair or lifting a dog bowl, were difficult for me. Christie had quickly learned to be my very efficient helper, and this had continued until her last illness and death from cancer. Working with her had opened my eyes to just how much could be achieved with a dog, given the right training. After she died in 2003 I'd had two hip replacement operations, fortunately both successful, but had really missed the loyal support of a dog while I was recovering. Now, almost two years later, I was fully fit and flexible and once again able to enjoy the long, rambling walks we had both loved so much.

Looking back even further, I remembered acquiring my very first Newfoundland, Cassie, over twenty-six years before. My three sons were still young children when she arrived, and one of my happiest memories is of them all roaring with laughter as Cassie romped with them in the snow, pulling a sledge.

I'd decided a Newfoundland would be the ideal family pet for us when my beautiful Golden Retriever, Crispin, was fourteen and nearing the end of his life. He had been such a perfect dog that I knew, even though I wanted another dog, I could not bear to take on a Retriever again. He was simply irreplaceable. At the time, Fred was often away working and with three small boys to look after, I wanted a big, protective dog but not a real guard dog – this was, after all, to be a family pet and had to be friendly and loving. I also wanted a working dog that I could train. I'd always admired the look of Newfoundlands and so set about researching the breed.

They are often described as 'gentle giants', and there's much debate about where they originate. Some experts believe they are descended from Viking bear dogs or else nomadic Native American dogs; others that they are related to Labradors as the two breeds share many of the same characteristics – both are sociable, intelligent dogs who are usually very willing to learn. They are also equally at home in the water, with the same oily, water-repellent coat and Newfoundlands even have webbed feet!

Whatever their origins, they have a long history. There are stories from the 1700s of Newfoundlands in Canada helping fishermen haul in their nets, carrying boat lines to shore, and retrieving anything or anyone who fell overboard. Lord Byron's faithful dog, Boatswain was a Newfoundland, as was Nana in *Peter Pan* and Bobby Kennedy's dog, Brumus. To ensure I was making the right choice I read masses, visited various breeders and also went along to the Newfoundland Water Trials to watch these swimming dogs in action. Everything I saw convinced me of the wisdom of my choice, and in the years since I've never regretted it. I've found the characters of each of my Newfoundlands to be quite different, they are always real individuals, but equally lovable.

Reassured by these thoughts, I realised we were driving along familiar lanes near our cottage in Sussex. The car slowed and Fred turned into the long winding drive which leads to our cottage. I gently woke Connie, smiling to myself at the prospect of getting to know her and training a new puppy again.

We were back early enough for Connie to explore her new home – or just part of it at this early stage. I had decided to introduce her first to the kitchen and utility room, where she would be sleeping, for I've found that having too many different rooms to investigate, too soon, can be confusing for a puppy. Excitement often leads to accidents where you least want them, especially for really young puppies who are not yet house trained.

Connie seemed to approve of her new home. Bright and alert, her tail wagging continuously, she soon confidently ventured into the garden, where she very conveniently weed. I said, 'Spend penny,' in encouraging tones as she performed, so that she would begin to associate the action with the words and enjoy the lavish praise afterwards. Experience has taught me that it's never too early to begin training, as bad habits, which are later very hard to break, can develop from day one.

I was determined that bedtime should be a pleasant experience for Connie. A generously sized puppy pen had been especially made for her. It was large enough for her bed to go at one end, with a few toys and space for her water bowl, opposite a distinct paper-lined toilet area at the other. Connie had plenty of time to wander freely in and out of the house and explore her new surroundings that first evening. I still remember how tiny she looked and how huge her pen appeared on that first day.

I am very aware of how worrying and lonely the first nights in their new home can be for puppies. This is after all the first time they have been away from their mother and the comfort of familiar surroundings. It's easy to forget that we, their new owners, are complete strangers who have whisked them away to an interesting but alien environment. It's no wonder many puppies cry and get quite distraught during these early nights. This has never seemed to me the best way to start a relationship which should properly be based on mutual affection and trust.

My solution was to make myself a temporary bed close beside Connie's pen, so that I could talk to her and sleep with my hand through the bars, to stroke and comfort her. After biscuits in bed, a ritual we still continue, she curled up contentedly and was soon sleeping soundly.

Our arrangement seemed to work well. We both slept peacefully. Each night after that I moved my bed just a little further away from her pen until my feet were in the guest room next-door, with my head near her. The next step was to retreat gradually across the guest room until I was actually able to sleep in the bed. I was almost out of her sight but I left the door open so Connie would have the reassurance of knowing I was still nearby.

Before very long I was back upstairs in my own bedroom to keep my now lonely husband company, and my now settled puppy was sleeping happily alone in the security of her own bedroom pen.

2

Getting to know Connie

When confronted with an adorably fluffy puppy only a few weeks old, it is very easy to fall into the trap of delaying its training. It is, however, vital to start this straight away. One of the first things I wanted to teach Connie was to feel happy and relaxed when left alone for short periods. The danger of postponing this lesson is clear. Eventually it will be necessary for you to leave your dog alone, and if this happens suddenly the puppy will panic all the more, often reacting with a frenzy of destructiveness and crying. I had recently helped with a poor young Spaniel who became so distraught whenever he was left alone, that he scratched the door frantically and made his paws bleed. I really did not want anything like this to happen to Connie.

I find baby gates are very useful at this stage, as puppies can learn to be on their own while still having the comfort of seeing you and consequently not feeling too isolated. In fact, baby gates are just as useful later on, if a dog is covered in mud or visitors are not quite sure whether they want a close encounter with a large, enthusiastic Newfoundland. I like a dog to be adaptable. There is nothing better than having your dog with you all the time but that is not always practical so I wanted Connie to be quite relaxed whenever she had to be alone, confident that I would come back to her before long. I started very gradually by dropping a few tasty pieces of her food on the floor, disappearing out of the door while she was eating it and then returning before she had barely noticed my absence. She soon became accustomed to me vanishing out of sight or closing a door behind me, especially as this was often accompanied by something interesting to eat. Another trick I used was to chat to her or even sing as I went further away, so that she knew I was still around. She was always quiet when I left, perhaps hoping I would go even further so she couldn't hear me at all!

House rules were the next thing to be introduced. Connie and I had to come to an agreement about what exactly was allowed. Everyone in the household was involved in this, and I briefed any visiting family and friends. It's very easy to allow a cute little puppy to curl up on the sofa, but altogether more tricky to stop a much larger, muddy dog from doing the same thing a few months later. They just won't understand what they've done wrong.

There was to be no barking or scratching at doors to be let in, either. At first, Connie pottered happily in the garden with me watching through the French windows. When she decided it was time to come inside, she would jump up, barking, and scrabble at the glass for attention. I would casually keep my eyes down, taking absolutely no notice of her. This would puzzle her and she'd sit down for a moment, to work out her next plan of action. At the point when she was sitting quietly, I would immediately open the door and she would come inside looking very pleased with herself. I could almost see her thinking, Ah-ha, that's trained her to do as I say. I only have to sit looking angelic and she lets me in at once. Brilliant, I will remember that next time.

This rather crafty method of training, where the dog is led to believe she is the one training you, has always worked very well for me. I also used it to discourage Connie from jumping up at the door excitedly whenever we were about to go out. I would ignore her until she sat down – at which point the door opened as if by magic. I suspect she became convinced it was the 'sit' which actually opened the door!

There were quite a few more rules for Connie to learn as soon as possible in these early days.

Early rules for happy dogs and happy owners

Dog don'ts

Do not come up to the table when we are eating, you will not get anything. If, however, you sit by the dishwasher, there might be a tasty treat when we have finished.

Do not try to go upstairs. This is bad for a young puppy. It caused big problems later when I needed Connie to go up and down flights of steps.

Do not paw at people. With young grandchildren Connie's paw would soon be on the same level as their faces as she grew bigger, I also have older relations and scratches on their legs would be very nasty. It is a natural thing for a puppy to paw at its mother so I knew I would have to be tactful with this one. The exception to the rule was when she was asked to lift one paw then the other for drying and grooming. Being so bright she very quickly learnt this and enjoyed all the extra fuss she had at these times.

11

Do not climb on the furniture. (This was easy to reinforce as I would sit on the floor to cuddle her.)

Do not jump up at anyone. (This was more difficult to teach but cunning tactics usually worked: I'd offer her something suitable to carry which made jumping up awkward. I remember she was particularly keen to carry her baby blanket or an old slipper.)

Do not chew furniture, humans, their possessions or hands!

Human dos

It seemed only fair that in return I was clear what my side of the bargain entailed:

I decide what we will do and when we do it, but I promise to make it fun and enjoyable for you.

I own all the toys. These will be stored in various toy boxes which you will be given at different times. The contents will be very exciting with a range of toys, some for playing, some for chewing.

I promise always to be fair, and any instructions I give will be clear and simple.

I will not get cross, confuse, worry or frighten you. If you do not understand something, I must realise it is my mistake, not yours.

Most importantly, you should enjoy life.

November is one of my least favourite times of the year. It always seems to me a dismal and invariably damp month, not quite a distinct season. It is not yet bright and frosty, there isn't the novelty of snow or any of the excitement of Christmas and all its festive preparations. The only arrivals are unwelcome ones – earwigs which hide in cereal packets, only to appear swimming around in my bowl once I've poured on the milk, and huge daddy-long-legs which flitter haphazardly around the kitchen and then seem to make a beeline for whatever I happen to be cooking. Even the robin's song sounds different at this melancholy time.

However, this year I was busy enjoying the company of my new puppy, watching her explore her surroundings and enjoy life. We spent ages sitting on the floor together on one of her soft beds, with Connie snuggled up beside me. She loved to lie there being cuddled while I held the end of a chew stick for her.

Connie was remarkably sweet-natured and calm. She reminded me in temperament of Crispin, my lovely Golden Retriever, who had also been unusually sensible for a young puppy. After a few days we allowed Connie into the sitting-room, on a lead at first, and soon could all enjoy peaceful evenings in front of the log fire. She was wonderfully adaptable. If I wanted to be quiet, she was happy to lie draped companionably across my lap but if we suddenly wanted to rush off, she was instantly up with a quick shake, alert and ready for anything. As we usually sat together on one of her beds in the evening, when it was time for Fred and me to go to ours, I simply gathered up my sleepy, floppy puppy and popped her into her pen, with her still-warm bedding to comfort her.

There were also new people for Connie to meet at home, although it would still be some weeks before she could go out to socialise properly. She had already met Barry on our initial trip to see her. He lives only a few miles away from us and was consequently her first visitor at home. She seemed delighted to see him again, wagging her tail frantically, which prompted him to look at her rather critically.

'I think she was finished off in a hurry and her tail's been stuck on in the wrong place,' my son laughed. 'It's also too short! Perhaps they ran out of material.' He made such a fuss of her though that, oblivious to his rude comments, Connie happily waggled the offending article so hard it looked as though she might shake it loose.

The next visitor keen to meet the new addition to the family was our youngest son, David. He arrived on his motorbike in full leather cycle gear after a long, chilly ride. Connie took one look at this strange apparition, with a round shining helmet where his head should be – and piddled all over the floor. Not being of a nervous disposition usually she quickly recovered, and watched fascinated as the alien creature removed the helmet and metamorphosed into a friendly human who obligingly knelt down on all fours to have his ears thoroughly washed.

Connie's first proper outing was to the vet for immunising injections and to be thoroughly checked over. I am lucky to have had the same wonderful vet looking after my dogs for many years now, and I knew she would be fine with him. Not all our early trips were quite so successful, though. We live in such a rural area that a vehicle is essential for socialising and all the normal hustle and bustle of life, so it was very important that Connie should be happy on car rides. On one practice run I carefully lifted her into the back of the car where she had a cardboard box with her familiar bedding inside, surrounded by her training toilet paper. I confidently set off for the short trip but had not reached the end of the lane before I noticed a horrible smell which was getting stronger. I glanced round and to my horror saw the back of the car was splattered with runny poo. Back home we went.

Next time I set off feeling relatively confident. What had happened before was just an unfortunate accident, unlikely to be repeated … It wasn't. This time Connie piddled everywhere, again before we'd reached the end of the lane. Never one to give up easily, I kept up my practice runs but made them very short, simply to the end of the drive at first, then into the lane where I immediately stopped and let her out to wee. Eventually we were able to reach the next lane without mishap – a triumphant five minute journey – before I had to let her out. Gradually, Connie relaxed and after that there were no more accidents in the car.

As she grew we were able to explore beyond the confines of the garden and walk further together. One of my favourite places is our little wood, adjoining the cottage. Connie and I began playing Hide and Seek there, with me running away to crouch down behind a tree out of sight, waiting for her to find me. She found this great fun from the start and it helped to teach her always to keep track of me. I was so lucky to have somewhere safe for her to play freely at such a young age. At the same time she was learning to walk to heel on a lead. I always took along a squeaky toy and played games to keep her attention on me and the toys rather than the lead. This was working well and soon we were both enjoying our walks together.

Playtime was another important part of Connie's day. When one of the toy boxes appeared she grew instantly animated and eager to join in. She quickly grew to understand that if she brought me back a toy, I would swap it for another even more thrilling than the first, or perhaps a tasty treat. As well as her toys, she was also encouraged to bring me the shoes or socks I had left on the floor.

'Clever girl, Connie. Pick it up,' I would say encouragingly as she snuffled intently around all the shoes lined up in the hall. Finding my fascinating scent on one, she would pounce happily. This was the tricky part. It was a great temptation for her to race away with the shoe, chomping on it as she went. But, being clever and very greedy, she soon realised it was worth bringing it to me instead. The quicker she brought it, the quicker she was praised and in return received a worthy reward. The ultimate prize was a treat from what I call the 'goodies pot', a small plastic bowl which was kept in the fridge, containing highly prized treats such as little pieces of chicken. An excited shout of 'Goodies pot!' and the sound of me tapping on it, would always bring a small black furball hurtling towards me. This has never failed. That wonderful pot still works like magic!

As I mentioned before, Newfoundlands have webbed feet and love water. It was not long before Connie discovered her innate water instincts and, like both my Newfoundlands before her, found it a great game to 'dig' in her water bowl. She'd splash puddles of water everywhere before triumphantly flinging both bowl and any remaining water across the floor. If she did this outside it was not too much of a problem, except for the fact that she then had no water left to drink. I tried to counter her game by cunningly surrounding the bowl with bricks, thinking that would deter her. No such luck. If anything it made it more of a sport as she soon found she could scrape the bricks away then carry on with her game unhindered. Indoors, I found

I was constantly mopping up great pools of water and refilling her bowl. In the end we reached something of a compromise. I rather unsportingly bought a very heavy china bowl that she could not pick up and placed it on a large tray. Connie continued to splash about in the bowl but at least most of the water now stayed in the tray.

Basic training was generally going well. Connie was obviously very intelligent and quick to learn, and from the start we seemed to understand one another. Within a few weeks she had found out how to pick up her little food bowl and bring it back to me, which was quite an achievement for such a baby. Most puppies, having eaten their food, will try to find an extra morsel by chewing the bowl or else taking it back to their bed, where they happily demolish it as it smells and tastes so delicious.

I encouraged Connie to pick up her bowl as this was what she wanted to do anyway. 'Pick up,' I would say excitedly, running to the sink. She thought it fun to chase after me, carrying her bowl. I then gently took the food bowl from her, saying, 'Give.' At the same time, in return I gave her a few more pieces of her food. I could see her thinking, 'Brilliant! Take bowl to the sink and mum gives me even more – her training is going well.' These key commands, 'Pick up' and 'Give', were to be two of the most important in the future.

At that early stage her fluffy baby coat was relatively easy to look after. When she was covered in mud, which was often, it was simple enough to pop her in the bath and clean her up. She was still small enough for me to pick her up, but was already growing fast. I have always preferred to sit on the floor to groom my dogs rather than use a special grooming table. It seems safer and easier to me. I knew that when Connie's dense, adult coat grew longer it would require a great deal more work to maintain, so

17

short sessions now on her baby fur would get her used to the idea of grooming.

It was now early December and as Connie was fully immunised I decided it was time to try out the local ring-craft club. Although she was used to meeting people, she had not yet met many other dogs. However, she was generally so friendly and calm that I was quietly confident. On the night of her first visit I hesitated outside the door to the local hall. Connie began sniffing excitedly, her ears alert at the unmistakable sound of lots of other dogs tantalisingly close, just the other side of that door.

'Steady now, Connie,' I said hopefully, pushing it open. With that she lurched enthusiastically forward and there was no stopping her.

Dragging me along behind, she forgot everything she had learned at home in her wild excitement. As I paid for the class, trying to juggle bag, purse and lead, Connie jumped up at the table, scattering paperwork, money and raffle tickets, wrecking the once neat display. Desperately trying to help clear up the mess, I managed to drop the bag containing her treats. As they scattered across the floor, there was a happy scrum of greedy dogs, including my own, gobbling up the goodies. By now thoroughly enjoying the mayhem, my sweet, gentle puppy obviously considered the whole idea of a dog club hilarious and, overcome with high spirits, pulled me from person to person, flinging herself at them in joyous abandon. So much for all my careful training of her. Though to be fair, it was a totally new experience for her.

By the time the ring-craft classes stopped for the Christmas break, Connie had begun to calm down a little and was slightly less over-enthusiastic. We had just passed our first important test, which was to collect a cup of tea and a biscuit and walk steadily across the hall to a seat wedged between other dog owners and their dogs, where I successfully managed to drink the tea without spilling any and eat most of the biscuit.

Christmas that year seemed particularly special. Of course we had our delightful new puppy and the whole family came to stay too, including Barry and David, and our middle son, Michael, his partner Nathalie and our two grandchildren, Tom and Lili. They all loved seeing Connie, and she for her part thought they were wonderful, especially the children, though the downside was that she longed to wash them all over and play rough-and-tumble games. She still needed to learn how to be gentle with them. I found the baby gates invaluable for keeping children and puppy safe and happy.

Christmas morning meant presents for everyone, including Connie. She loved being allowed to rip off the paper and thoroughly enjoyed her big squeaky Christmas cracker and delicious chew sticks, which kept her out of too much mischief while we were all busy.

To my delight, the New Year brought the winter's first downfall of snow. Connie, now four months old, rushed outside and skidded to a halt in amazement. She gambolled about, burying her nose experimentally in the cold white frosting, shaking snowflakes from her fur. We set off for the wood at a run. The trees were weighed down with snow, the bracken below a tracery of white. Even the tangled brambles looked like works of art, with their arched stems etched glistening white in the sun. Connie used her nose to explore this strange new world while I marvelled at the animal and bird tracks criss-crossing the woodland paths. The stream trickling down through the gully looked especially magical, bubbling between the snow-covered hummocks of ferns and grasses to either side.

After lunch Fred and I climbed up through our wood, over the stile and through the fields to the top of the hill. Connie's young legs could just manage the walk, though she was puzzled by the icy balls of snow which gathered between the pads of her paws. It was so beautiful at the top, looking back over the peaceful rural valley, the snow-covered fields gleaming in the winter sunshine. The lines of the South Downs were clear and dramatic that day, very different from their more usual soft, indistinct outlines. Connie joined us as we stood drinking in the sight, her dark coat flecked with icy crystals. 'Good girl,' I said softly, stroking her head. I felt so happy and content on such a perfect day with Connie beside us.

3

The Best-laid Plans

The New Year snow soon melted and life returned to normal. I began to make plans for the year ahead, as I tend to each January. In the spring Connie would be old enough to go to dog shows. We might even try obedience competitions which, judging from her early training, she could prove to be suited to. I was also looking forward to beginning water work with her. There are so many things you can do with a Newfoundland and I've always wanted my dogs to enjoy a range of different activities so that they never become bored.

Ring-craft classes resumed and Connie and I returned for the first lesson of 2006. I was surprised by how much stronger she seemed to have become over the Christmas holiday, and after that evening I felt very stiff. The following day, Connie rushed about playing as I gathered up the dead leaves that had fallen over the winter months, piling them into huge mounds. It was hard work if nothing exceptional, but yet again I felt unusually stiff and tired that evening.

Next day Fred, Connie and I set off to see my brother Derek and sister-in-law Stella. They have a sweet-tempered elderly Welsh Springer Spaniel called Trampus who is such a dignified gentleman I thought he would be ideal to teach

Connie how to behave with more mature dogs. They live by the sea and after lunch we all walked along the beach. This was the first time Connie had seen the sea and she loved it, although she was a little wary of the waves chasing her on the shore. We scrambled back up the shingle and went inside for tea and buns. My plan was then to visit Aunt Joy, who lived nearby.

I tried to stand up but found my legs gave way beneath me. I must have overdone things in the garden yesterday. Nothing to worry about, I decided. I'd probably pulled a muscle in my back. My brother offered to drive me to my aunt's house but, much to my annoyance, I then found I could not get my shoes on. Growing increasingly impatient with myself, I settled for Wellington boots. With the benefit of hindsight, I see now that I should have realised that something was very wrong. Instead I persevered, although getting into the car was tricky. Getting out was even worse. I needed help from both Derek and my aunt taking off my boots, and felt decidedly strange. My poor aunt had been in hospital until recently after a bad fall and was still using a walking frame to get about, yet *she* was more mobile than I was. That afternoon it seemed quite funny and I remember the three of us laughing about it. When we arrived back at Derek and Stella's house, Fred, who had waited behind with Connie, was surprised to see me obviously in pain and barely able to move.

We set off for home. Tomorrow was 19 January, our son Michael's birthday. I was optimistically certain I would feel better then. Luckily I had no idea that almost a year would pass before I felt well or normal again.

That night I slept only fitfully and I'll never forget waking up the next morning. The pain was indescribable. At that point, however, I still wasn't taking things too seriously. I was sure this was only a temporary blip and that my back would soon right itself; after all, I was generally healthy. Yes, I'd had the hip replacement operations a couple of years earlier, but I'd made a good recovery. Fred phoned the doctor who suggested taking Co-codamol to ease the pain and inflammation. If things didn't improve in a few days, I should go in to see him. As a rule I don't take many medicines, and as I don't suffer from headaches and had never had any back pain before this, I hardly ever took painkillers. Maybe that was why the tablets had such a pronounced effect on me. They didn't seem to ease the pain very much but they made me feel dreadful and I started to be violently sick. Poor Connie didn't know what was going on. Neither did Fred – even after my operations and through childbirth, I hadn't been this bad.

Unfortunately, it all coincided with our oil tank being replaced. As I was lying on the floor groaning and there was general confusion, Fred, who is usually so careful and organised, didn't really watch what was happening. As a result, we got our new tank but since it would not fit into the same position as the old one, it was plonked down in completely the wrong place and later we had to fork out a considerable sum to have it moved. At the time, I really didn't care!

Fred looked after me, cooking and cleaning the house as well as working at his own job, but I began to worry about the effect my illness was having on Connie. She was still so young and such a sensitive puppy, I knew the sight of me in agony could be very distressing for her and didn't want it to have a permanent effect. I hesitated for a few days but my back still showed no sign of improvement and, after much deliberation, we decided the best thing was for Connie to go away until I was better. In the past, my old dogs had occasionally stayed at a nearby kennels I completely trusted. The owners looked after all their boarding dogs extremely well and I knew Connie would be safe and loved there. This was not ideal but it seemed the best solution and, after all, I was still certain this was only a temporary problem and I would soon be fit again.

And so, on 26 January, Fred took my sweet Connie away. I was supposed to see the doctor that day but had to cancel the appointment as I was just too sick to venture out. When I finally made it to the surgery, my doctor was unsure what exactly was causing the problem, but recommended rest and more of the dreaded painkillers. By the beginning of February I was feeling a little better, well enough to walk slowly outside with a stick. It was wonderful to get out and feel more mobile again. I thought it might be possible for Connie to come home and was longing to see her. Perhaps I tried to do too much, too soon. The back problem was still affecting my legs and I stumbled on the brick doorstep, falling heavily on to my back and in an instant dashing any hopes I'd had of a speedy recovery. So began what was to become one of the worst periods of my life.

There were endless visits to the doctor and hospital as well as trips to the physiotherapist. What I remember most clearly is lying between the rows of chairs in waiting rooms as it was simply impossible for me to sit in a chair. March was the worst month. It saw me rushed to hospital in the middle of the night, screaming from a pain so excruciating that I didn't even feel embarrassed when the two ambulancemen had to sit me on the loo. At the time, I barely noticed. I was more worried about being strapped to a stretcher in the ambulance when I was vomiting constantly. One of the ambulancemen reassured me he would keep watch. Later, during the journey, he hardly inspired confidence when I glanced across to see him fast asleep. After this nightmare episode I was admitted to hospital for a few days of X-rays and scans, to try to determine exactly what was causing the problem. While I was there even morphine injections didn't ease the agony I suffered.

I will never forget the terrible days after my discharge from hospital. There was nothing more that could be done to help me, apparently. The pain was unrelenting although I was taking the maximum dose of painkillers. One bedtime was the worst. While attempting to undress, I suffered the most horrendous spasm of agony, far worse than anything I had experienced before. Barely able to breathe, I collapsed on to the bed. At that moment life seemed unbearable to me. I felt I couldn't cope with this pain any longer. Exhausted and sobbing, I forced myself to breathe calmly and relax. I thought of Fred and my family, and Connie, of course. I had so much to live for, somehow I had to carry on and get through this.

Throughout this time my body was still reacting badly to the painkillers and, as I could hardly eat because of the pain, my weight had dropped dramatically until I weighed little more than six stone. No one seemed to know exactly what was causing the problem. There were several false diagnoses because of my history of hip problems. One duty doctor I saw was neither sympathetic nor tactful. I never cry in public but he quickly reduced me to tears by bluntly telling me that I was likely to remain in my current state for a year. There was no reassurance from him, no hint that things might improve or I might regain even a little mobility any time soon.

Devastated, I sat alone in my hospital room and thought back to the beginning of the year, just a few short months ago, when I had felt so hopeful and life was full of exciting plans. And what of Connie now? There was no way I could keep her, it was just not fair. She was a young and energetic puppy while I could hardly move. I would be unable to lean over to groom or even pet her. It would be impossible for me to care for her. Tears streamed down my face at the thought of giving her up.

And what of our home? It was hardly suitable for an invalid, and how could Fred possibly manage it all on his own? Victorian weather-boarding needed regular painting and maintenance. Then there were the gardens and my beloved wood. It was carpeted with bluebells in the spring and had a small, natural pond fringed by daffodils which was a haven for wildlife. The pond overflowed into a miniature stream that trickled down through the wood in a series of mini waterfalls. Connie already loved playing there while I worked clearing the thickets of bracken and brambles. Fred and I had lived there for most of our married life, always working together. Everything I had ever prized in my life seemed impossible for me now.

Just as I was feeling most sorry for myself, a nurse came in to check on me. I found myself resenting her fitness and the fact that she was free to walk about. Unlike the specialist I'd seen, though, she took time to talk to me and, to my amazement, told me that only a few months before she'd had a similar problem with her back and been confined to a wheelchair. But here she was now, fit to work. She advised me not to make any big decisions at this point, and most importantly, gave me much encouragement and cause for hope. From that moment on, I was determined to do everything I could to regain my old life, to keep our home and, above all, Connie.

After lots of false trails, countless X-rays, scans and hospital visits, I finally saw a back specialist who could explain what was happening to me. The trouble was basically a severe problem with a damaged disc which had been exacerbated by my fall and the fact that my spine was also showing the wear and tear of age, with some evidence of crumbling. But at least now I had a diagnosis, along with acupuncture and physiotherapy to help ease some of the symptoms, although they did nothing for the pain.

At home, lying in bed fighting the pain and side effects of the medication, I had plenty of time to think. Connie was still at the kennels, which was hardly an ideal situation. Luckily, there were fields there where the dogs romped and played together, which would be brilliant for her canine socialisation, but she really needed to be out and about, seeing different places and people. I'd had such plans for her training, and we would have continued with ring-craft classes. It was all too easy to drift back into depression and despair in those days, but I had to focus on the future and try to be positive.

Throughout this miserable period, I was in too much pain and far too sick and exhausted to see visitors. I was still taking masses of pills and couldn't lift my arms to undress or bend down to pull on my socks. But when I was feeling a little better, my wonderful sister-in-law Stella came to see us. She knew how busy Fred had been looking after me, and brought us a shepherd's pie. I'd had little appetite and had lost a lot of weight by then as it was such an effort to eat lying down. But as Stella lifted the shepherd's pie from the Aga, a delicious smell wafted through the house and reached my bed. I still remember how inviting it looked, bubbling and topped with golden mashed potato. For the first time in weeks I ate hungrily and, to her delight and Fred's great relief, I asked for more. Afterwards there was an orange which Fred had carefully divided into segments. I remember thinking that my husband was certainly taking to heart the 'in sickness' part of our wedding vows. I also reflected on the way he had always accepted that along with me, he would be taking on a dog – six of them, in fact, over the years – as well as a variety of other animals. I was very grateful for his tolerance and never more so than during those endless months.

Even at the darkest points, I tried to plan for Connie's return and how I might continue training her. I kept focussing on this thought and it really helped me to keep going. All my experience with dogs and the work I had done with them throughout my life seemed to have been preparing me for this challenge. I kept remembering Christie, my previous Newfoundland, and how helpful she had been to me when I was quite immobile before my hip replacements. The more I thought about it, the more convinced I became that not only could I carry on training Connie, from my bed if necessary, but that she could be a positive help to me too as I slowly recovered.

4

A Country Childhood

Lying immobile in bed left only my mind free and I found myself looking back over a lifetime spent working with dogs. I tried to remember where it had all started and realised I had to go back to my very earliest memories. My whole life had been spent with dogs and other animals, in the countryside I loved so much.

I was born on 12 December 1938, sixteen and a half months after my brother Derek. My mother had been an actress and my father was a barrister, though I hardly knew him. Unusually for the times, my parents divorced when I was very small and we lived with my maternal grandparents in Portsmouth. With the outbreak of war, my family moved to the small hamlet of West Harting in West Sussex on the north side of the Downs. My earliest memories are of my life there. It is where my story really begins.

I think it was happy memories of the cottage we lived in there that first drew me to our current home. Whereas this cottage is weather-boarded in the Kentish style, my childhood home was built of stone and flint. The walls were almost a metre thick, and it looked exactly as a child would draw a house: two windows on top, two below, and a door in the middle with roses beside it, climbing and tumbling their way up to the bedroom windows. I still can conjure up their heady, soft scent. A flagstone path led up to the front door, then wound its way round to the garden behind.

Outside the back door was a well with a metal bucket used to draw up water. The well head was always kept securely covered. As a treat, Mother would lift this cover and, holding us tightly by the hand, allow Derek and me to peer down past the wet cut-brick walls which seemed to go on for ever to the water below. Less appealingly, a kitten once managed to creep under the cover and sadly drowned when it fell into the water. The well was so deep there was no way to retrieve the poor little thing. This did not deter anyone from drinking the water – these were practical times and, with no other supply to the cottage, there was no alternative. I don't seem to remember anyone being any the worse as a result.

The lavatory was also outside, way down the flagstone path. It was wooden with a tiled roof and two loos, one adult-sized wooden seat set next to a child-sized one. With no mains drainage, beneath the seats stood two large, smelly buckets. There were several knotholes in the wood which made it even more draughty, and as a small boy Derek thought it a great game to peer through one of the holes, conveniently set at his eye level whenever adults were in residence.

The garden was surrounded by several hedges, including one which ran around my grandfather's vegetable patch. He cycled over from Portsmouth, or maybe from the station at Petersfield, each Friday for the weekend and for holidays. He continued to lecture at the college in Portsmouth, knowing the rest of the family were safe from any bombing raids in the cottage.

As was usual for the times, the front door was never used. It remained bolted shut with a big blanket hanging in front to keep out the draughts. Downstairs there were two main rooms, a little sitting-room which was used as a bedroom at first for my grandparents, then later after the war for Derek, and the kitchen-cum-living-room. This was the heart of the house and most things were done there. The range in the living-room provided the only real heating and was also used for baking pies and stews and general cooking. There was a single storey scullery behind the living-room where we had a primus stove and where buckets of water from the well were stored. The wireless was kept in the living-room, and in pride of place stood a long heavy oak table. There was also a divan bed which acted as a sofa and somewhere for guests to sleep.

My grandparents had four children and on high days and holidays, like Christmas, there could be as many as nine adults and seven children all staying in our little cottage. During the summer tents would be pitched outside in the garden and various cousins and aunts and uncles would sleep there.

Besides having no running water, we had no electricity. Oil lamps and candles provided our lighting, casting long shadows and pools of soft yellow light. An oil lamp always stood on the kitchen table and each day had to be carefully cleaned, the glass chimney wiped free from soot and the brass base refilled with oil. At bedtime we carried dish-shaped blue enamel candlesticks set with white candles up the stairs to bed with us. I still associate candlelight with feeling cosy and safe, sleepily snuggled beneath the blankets and eiderdown as my mother sang to us or made up a bedtime story. The white blankets had narrow borders of colour and I liked to pick at these lines of blue, green and pink, and keep the coloured fluff in a matchbox.

After a short holiday away with my grandparents, Derek and I returned home to find that Mother had created an

31

inside bathroom of sorts, not that anyone would view it as such today. She had painted a small pantry-sized room pink, adding a lidded bucket and chamber pots and a tin basin for washing. She had even painted the backs of the wooden toothbrushes! Bathtime, however, still meant the tin bath in front of the range, filled with kettles and pans of hot water heated on the stove. Looking back, I realise just how hard my mother worked. But whatever she did, she always looked happy, singing and laughing over the endless washing, and she's still the only person I've ever seen who made scrubbing a floor look fun.

Food was stored on the mantelpiece shelf above the range, out of reach of the field mice that took shelter and free meals where they could particularly in the autumn when the weather turned colder.

There was a definite pattern to the meals we ate and it is not hard to this day for me to conjure up the memory of those wonderful home cooking smells. Always a roast on Sunday, then mince with the leftover meat on Monday – it was a great treat to be allowed to turn the handle of the mincer, adding cold roast meat then bread to bulk out the mince.

My grandmother always seemed to be baking, especially apple pies. She would give Derek and me a piece of light-coloured pastry each and it was a family joke to see just how dirty my portion became before I eventually got round to eating it. Living in the country with our own chickens meant we were never short of eggs and we even sent boxes regularly to family members in Bournemouth. The summer months meant a flurry of activity in our kitchen-cum-living-room with furry gooseberries, and sharp redcurrants and blackcurrants all being bottled to preserve them through the long winter months ahead. Grandfather also grew and stored potatoes, sprouts and peas.

Beyond the garden and hedges were fields and farmland. Although we rented the cottage and garden, my grand-parents had bought the field and old barn behind the cottage. Even as a small child, I longed to be able to keep my own pony there. My interests were always firmly focussed on animals and I remember quite clearly planning and scheming about how I would care for this lovingly imagined pony.

This field was the setting for one of our childhood games which went badly wrong and still features in my night-mares. It was towards the end of a long dry summer – seemingly typical of my childhood and yet so rare now! We, or most likely Derek, had found a box of matches and it seemed harmless fun to build a small bonfire. The long grass in the field was tinder-dry and there was a warm but steady breeze blowing. To our horror, our small fire quickly took hold and spread until the flames began to lick towards the crumbling old barn and its bales of straw. Somehow we managed to put out the blaze. No one was hurt and there was no lasting damage but even now, sixty years later, I'm still watchful and cautious whenever we have bonfires.

Derek was a lively athletic boy and I, as a younger, rather plump and timid girl, was something of a disap-pointment to him. He was always trying to encourage me to play cricket with him in the lane or to race about on some madcap game he'd invented. He also teased me mercilessly, hiding my beloved toys in the coal house and tugging on my long plaits. At his instigation, when we were alone in the cottage we tried using our bubble pipes like real ones, filling them with brown paper and setting them alight. I can still remember the distinctive taste of soap, smoke and brown paper.

One Christmas, I was given an old doll's pram which

my mother had painstakingly restored, replacing the hood lining and sewing matching covers for it. This pram was to feature in many of our games. It had a sturdy, well-made metal frame with springs, just like a miniature version of a proper child's one. It was certainly strong enough for both Derek and me to take the occasional ride in. One time, out in the lane, my brother jumped in and instructed me to give him a good hard push, the idea being that he would trundle on down the slope. I did as I was told, with surprisingly effective results. Derek and the pram gained momentum, hurtling downhill until the front wheel jolted against a large stone and promptly tipped my brother out on to the gravel. Both his knees were badly grazed and it took ages for my mother carefully to pick out all the tiny stones and bits of grit. I can't remember feeling particularly sorry for him at the time, though.

Derek also had his own toys and was particularly attached to Teddy and Bunny who travelled everywhere with him. One day we returned home after a day out and he realised to his horror that he had left the furry pair behind, sitting on the bus seat. My mother managed to speak to a conductor on another bus and word was passed on about the missing much-loved duo. The last bus of the day arrived in the village with Teddy and Bunny on board, and my mother, Derek and I were waiting at the bus stop to meet them.

Probably the most memorable thing my brother did was to fling himself from the bedroom window. Again my pram featured in the game. Derek suggested using it as a taxi, and parked it outside on the flagstone path just below my bedroom window. He then ran inside and proceeded to lob cushions and pillows out through the open window, to land in the pram below. He was so absorbed in this sport that finally he forgot to let go. To my open-mouthed surprise, the pillow with Derek still attached to it sailed out of the window and disappeared from view. One moment he was there and the next he had vanished. My grandparents were in the small sitting room below when a rather large object plummeted past the window. Looking out, they saw my brother lying dazed on the flagstones. Perhaps he was mildly concussed but there were no broken bones or long-term ill effects. I don't even recall anyone being unduly worried. I think he was checked by a doctor but there were certainly no hospital visits or X-rays – the story simply passed into our family history as another amusing anecdote.

Late-summer days were spent blackberrying in the nearby fields and hedgerows. We would take a picnic and return in the evening, laden with our spoils. When I went to bed the ripe berries would still be in our bowls and buckets, but when I woke next morning, as if by magic there would be rows of jars filled with blackberry jam and usually a pie still warm and fragrant. My mother always insisted the fairies had made them and for years I believed her, dreaming blackberry-scented dreams of them busily at work in our kitchen.

I loved the changing seasons, watching for primroses in the sunlit copse every spring and later for early-summer bluebells. In the midsummer my mother and I would rescue stranded baby birds, trying to rear them on bread and milk, not realising their parents would find them if we just let them be. One particularly cold winter, when the snow seemed to last for weeks, Derek built an igloo in the garden. We furnished it with two stools and a tiny table complete with a candle. Mother found us old tin trays to use as sledges and the three of us slid down the snowy banks together.

In summertime our hens would wander round happily

inside the cool of the house. This was my introduction to and the beginning of a lifelong interest in chickens. There was Fanny, a Rhode Island Red without a tail, and a Light Sussex called Betsy Ann, I remember. There always seemed to be chicks, which invariably grew up into cockerels. The Light Sussexes were particularly tame and I'd pick them up and take them for walks with me along the lanes. I still cringe with horror at the memory of a jolly neighbour arriving with his roll of long, sharp knives to dispatch one of my friendly chickens.

My mother and grandmother cooked up their own blend of chicken-feed on the range, concocted from leftovers and kitchen scraps and seasoned with pungent, aromatic spices. The scent as it cooked was wonderful and drew me in. Whenever I had the chance I would sample this hot concoction, savouring its delicious spiciness.

The war made little real impact on my life as we were so far out in the country but I do remember the air-raid sirens and having to shelter under the heavy oak kitchen table. Sometimes we were put to bed under it, with Derek lying on one side of the footrest running between the table legs and me lying on the other. As soon as my mother left, my brother would whisk off my covers. The grown-ups had to squeeze into the little cupboard under the stairs. For a long time I associated all aeroplanes with danger. Once, hearing a plane while playing with the chickens, I raced inside for shelter, only to be chased out again by a brood of hens who thought it a great game.

As well as the chickens there were always lots of cats and kittens around in the nearby farms. At the time it was not usual to neuter pets in the way it is now. One particularly beautiful grey and white kitten was to be mine and I deliberated long and hard before calling her Mary. When she grew older, it became obvious that she was a he, but

the name stuck. This early life also gave me my first introduction to dogs, for living with us during those war years
was my grandmother's roan Cocker Spaniel, Freckles. He
was amazingly co-operative, allowing me to dress him up
to play the Wolf to my Little Red Riding Hood. I knotted
a headscarf beneath his chin and thought he was most
convincing as the Wolf, although he never could manage
to be very frightening with his long ears lolling down at
the sides. I loved to sit stroking those long ears with fur
as soft as silk, which dangled into our buckets of drinking
water whenever he surreptitiously helped himself to a drink.
I also liked feeding him dog biscuits as a treat, making
sure I had my share too.

My grandmother would encourage Freckles to perform
all sorts of tricks. 'Die for Hitler!' she would say, and
Freckles would take no notice. Commanded to 'Die for
the King!', however, he would immediately roll over and
play dead, to my brother's and my delight. Grandma would
also shiver and say, 'I'm cold,' and Freckles would at once
trot off to close the door. This gave me the first inkling of
just how much it is possible to teach a dog.

No buses stopped at our small hamlet and so Grandma
walked to South Harting, the next village, to catch a bus
to Petersfield. Freckles always walked with her, and when
the bus arrived Grandma would tell him to go home,
which he always did. He instinctively seemed to know
what time the bus would arrive back and always set out
to meet it. Unfortunately Grandma sometimes missed her
usual bus and, if that happened, Freckles would simply
head home and set off once more an hour later to meet
her from the next bus. He also liked to roam and once
got lost. We looked everywhere with no luck. Eventually
he found his own way home but with a cruel gin trap for
catching rabbits on his leg. We were horrified to see him

dragging his injured leg along attached to the trap when he eventually managed to return home. Once free he soon recovered, looking a little thinner but otherwise none the worse for his adventure.

I remember on VE Day we all went on our bicycles to the village to join the celebration. I was given a little Union Jack flag to wave and loved the fact that Freckles was bought a red, white and blue ribbon which was tied in a bow on his collar. I was delighted by this and thought he looked lovely.

My mother worked as a teacher in the local village school in South Harting, cycling there and back with me perched behind her. Too young to go to school myself, I would be looked after by some of the older infants. Freckles would always come too, running along beside the bicycle. Once there, he spent his school day snoozing under Mum's desk until it was home time. My mother came to teach there rather by accident. My Aunt Rae was a qualified teacher and had originally been offered the position at the school. She was then offered another job much closer to her own home, which she accepted instead. As there were few telephones at the time, she asked my mother to let the headmaster at South Harting know as soon as possible. This my mother did and in the process so impressed the head that she was offered the job although she was not a qualified teacher at the time. She was to stay for thirty years.

Following my success in taking the young cockerels for a walk, I decided it was time to move on to other animals. At first I tried taking the cat. Using a piece of string for a collar and lead, I tried to pull Mary along, poor thing. Not surprisingly this did not work. I really wanted to take Freckles, but though I cajoled and pushed and pulled, he steadfastly refused to leave the garden for me. Force definitely did not work. Suddenly I had a brainwave. I raided the dog biscuit tin and laid a trail through the garden, out of the gate and along the lane. Returning, I showed Freckles the first biscuit. He needed no further encouragement and happily followed me out through the gate and along the lane. I had learned my first important lesson in animal behaviour: rewards work.

Freckles also taught me another vital but sad lesson about keeping a pet. He was already quite old when we moved to West Harting and eventually he died. My mother and grandmother carefully laid him in a basket in the pink-painted bathroom. He was covered with a blanket but I can still remember looking at his speckly paws peeping out from underneath the cover.

Although we had nothing to do with my father, we still saw my paternal grandparents, and Derek and I often stayed with them in their country house. Grandmother was an artist and an animal lover. In fact, she'd insisted on taking her six Yorkshire Terriers away with her on honeymoon! It would not be unfair to describe her as eccentric, and I have a suspicion that I am probably rather like her. I recall a dreadful row going on one morning, which was unusual. At the time, Grandmother had a Spaniel on whom she doted. She cleaned his teeth for him every day. By mistake, Grandfather had managed to use the dog's toothbrush to clean his own teeth. Quite how the brushes were mixed up I don't know but he was horrified, though not as appalled as my grandmother – worrying for her dog's health rather than her husband's! She threw away the toothbrush in disgust.

My grandmother also introduced me to horses. She had a friend who owned a pony and trap. I loved to feed the pony with sugar lumps and ride along in the trap. Like many young girls, I dreamed of owning a pony of my own.

I had riding lessons at a gloomy old house rather than a conventional riding school, practising on a pony called Snowy. I never saw anyone else there apart from my riding instructor, and rumour had it the house was haunted. It was even claimed that the local minister had exorcised the rambling building, ringing bells all around it and trying to persuade the ghosts to leave. Years later, when I was fourteen, Grandmother offered to buy me a pony of my own on condition that I find suitable stables. It was no easy task but I was very determined and kept looking until I found a farm at East Harting who could offer me a stable and field. Prince was a Dartmoor pony, 12½ hands high and what's known as a rig, which meant that he was only part-gelded. At first he was very frisky, rather bad-tempered and prone to kick, but with gentle perseverance he settled down and I loved riding him.

Our time at the cottage in West Harting came to an end when I was eight. I still look back on it with such affection. All these years later it seems to me to have been a magical time and place. Although my mother had been working as a teacher she had no qualifications. At the end of the war many intensive teacher training courses were set up and she decided she should take one. She would earn more if she qualified and her job would be more secure, but it was a very difficult decision to take. We had all been so happy in our life at the cottage and this would uproot everyone for eighteen months. She also had to decide what to do with us children, the chickens and cats.

In the end, the chickens came to live with me at my grandparents' house in Portsmouth but were kept in a small enclosed coop which seemed very sad when they had been used to roaming free. I wondered at the time what had happened to the cockerels, but with hindsight can guess now. Tommy, one of our cats, came too but disappeared shortly after the move. My grandmother and I walked the streets of the neighbourhood, searching for him, and I remember looking at the rows and rows of houses, the roads and pavements, and hating it all. I longed for our country cottage, the fields and the open space. A few weeks later, I too managed to lose myself. In West Harting I had been used to wandering about alone without any problems, but in Portsmouth everywhere looked the same and I had no clue as to where I was. A kindly lady tried to return me to the wrong family and I can still remember my feeling of utter panic. Crying bitterly, I did eventually find the right road and made my way back to my grandparents. Needless to say, I was far more cautious after that.

Derek, along with Mary the cat, stayed behind with the minister and his wife so that he could easily make the journey to Midhurst Grammar where he was now a pupil. I missed my mother dreadfully and longed to be with her. When she came home for holidays the anticipation and excitement always made me sick. We did occasionally visit her at college and, typically, my clearest memory is of a corgi there belonging to one of her friends which I was allowed to take for walks on a lead.

There were also holidays at my grandparents' other house by the sea at Felpham which I enjoyed, and stays at my aunt and uncle's farm where I felt very much at home. There were always kittens and calves to pet there as well as noisy flocks of ducks and geese. The goslings had the softest down and were wonderful to hold. My aunt and uncle also owned a massive but very gentle German Shepherd dog who was constantly getting into trouble for running along beside the railway line which crossed their fields and chasing the trains.

At the end of her college course my mother was offered her old job back at the village school in South Harting.

41

Sadly the cottage we'd loved so much was no longer free and along with the job Mother was given a council house in the village. There was nowhere else available. I never liked that house and to my shame now, remember how embarrassed I used to feel about living there.

We soon acquired a whole new menagerie of animals for our new home. Buying furniture from a house sale near my grandparents' home in Portsmouth, I saw and fell in love with a litter of Persian kittens. I had never before seen anything quite so exquisite or fluffy. I asked if we could buy one but of course they were far too expensive. Seeing how smitten I was, the family offered me a kitten from another litter of Siamese Persian crosses. And so Dinah came into my life. She had a small, pointed appealing Siamese face and long fluffy black fur. She lived with me for many years, having lots of litters. Derek and I also had a hamster each and the pair of them were constantly escaping, though they never went far. One morning my mother discovered mine sitting inside an Easter egg on her dressing table, delicately nibbling chocolate. I also kept goldfish and angora rabbits which I bred and sold. However, for me there was still one thing missing.

I longed for a dog of my own and badgered my poor mother dreadfully. Eventually, worn down by my insistent demands, she gave in. I'd given the choice of dog a great deal of consideration. I thought it would be wonderful to have a Rough Collie like Lassie, or perhaps a German Shepherd – they always seemed to be performing clever, courageous feats, at least in the movies. In the end, I followed the family tradition and we went to see a litter of Cocker Spaniel puppies. Sadly, when we arrived the breeder explained that they had all been sold, except for one who had injured itself running into a nail. Needless to say, my mother decided that was not suitable. I was so disappointed, but a few weeks later the breeder contacted us again to say that one of the male puppies had been returned and was now available. He did mention that the first owner had complained the puppy was bad-tempered and had bitten her child, which should have been a warning. However, as all the Cocker Spaniels in our family had had lovely temperaments, my mother wasn't worried by this and, much to my delight, agreed that I could have the puppy.

I decided the name Sandy was perfect for my beautiful golden-red Cocker Spaniel. At first it was wonderful to have my own puppy, but very soon Sandy began to demonstrate that his first owner had not exaggerated his bad temper. He was definitely in charge and terrorised my brother and me. If Sandy decided to sit on the sofa we dared not go near it as he would growl and threaten to bite us. If he had a bone, his favourite place to chew it was the middle of the living-room and, again, we were not allowed anywhere near. In fact, we were so frightened that if we wanted to move past him we would edge out of the back door, go round the house and back in through the front door. I can remember when mother was ill in bed once, the doctor called but could get nowhere near her as Sandy was on the bed, growling and threatening.

I had so looked forward to having a puppy of my own but found I was not enjoying the reality at all. Walks were a struggle with Sandy pulling hard on the lead like a traction engine, dragging me behind. If I held on to his collar he would try to bite my hand. As he grew from cute-looking (though not tempered) puppy into an adolescent, the aggression problems continued. He also developed what I later realised was Rage Syndrome, not uncommon in red Cocker Spaniels, where he would go into a trance-like state, eyes blazing and ready to attack, really biting hard if handled. He once bit my mother on the chest and I remember feeling horribly shocked at what my dog had done.

In many ways, looking back, I'm surprised we kept Sandy. I suppose neither my mother nor I liked to give up on an animal once we had accepted responsibility for it, and there was nowhere to go for advice. In those days there were no dog-training classes and certainly no dog behaviourists. Castration (which can sometimes help with aggression) was unheard of and vets were only seen for serious injuries and illness, so you simply managed alone.

As Sandy matured he gradually improved; the outbursts of aggression eventually stopped as did the Rage Syndrome, except for one very nasty incident. I had a pet rabbit called Benjamin and Sandy had always been completely trustworthy with him. However, one day we were minding my grandmother's latest young Spaniel and the two dogs together attacked and mauled my rabbit. I was extremely upset and it was a hard way to learn that, however well you know your own dog, you really cannot predict how two of them will behave together if left unsupervised.

By the time I was in my mid-teens, Sandy and I had become best friends and I had the affectionate companion I had dreamed of. Just like Freckles with my grandmother, he walked me to the school bus and then returned home alone. There were no dog wardens in those distant days and lone dogs were not considered strays. Together we walked the South Down trails and local woods. He came along with me on buses and trains, and always on holiday with the family to the seaside or a boat on the Norfolk Broads. When I rode my bicycle or pony, Prince, Sandy would run alongside, easily keeping up. I often cycled to the farm where I stabled Prince early in the morning, and had to remember to give Sandy a rolled up sack to carry, to stop him barking with excitement and waking everyone else.

One of my favourite haunts in the village was the black-smith's forge where I spent lots of time while my mother was at school preparing lessons. I couldn't resist the place. There were the horses to see, of course, but the smith also kept greyhounds and ferrets. I liked watching the bellows and fire, the smell and hiss when the horses were shod. Later, when I had my own pony, I took him there for shoes and I can still remember the banging of the hammer, long silent now of course.

Although my mother was a teacher and my brother always did very well at school, I struggled there and found learning difficult. My mother never quite got round to really teaching me and I hated school apart from the two pigs that were kept there for the boys' lessons. I became very adept at thinking up cunning excuses not to go. The only subject I really liked was English. Although it took me ages to learn to read fluently, once I properly started I was never without a book – usually something about animals. I was a regular at Petersfield Library, devouring everything on horses and riding, and adventure stories, especially if they featured a dog. Maths I never really got the hang of. I didn't altogether see the point of most of my school lessons and would much rather be outside with my pony or dog. However, I was finally given a reason to try harder. I had joined the Young Farmers' and I took part in many activities including cattle-judging, heavy horse work and debating. Through their meetings I came to hear about Brinsbury Training Farm which we visited for one of the public-speaking competitions. Brinsbury was a type of pre-college, offering courses for farmers. I was then fifteen and knew I wanted to work with animals. I thought I could go to Brinsbury and then maybe on to a farm institute for training. At my interview I was told to go away, pass some GCEs and then re-apply. This was just the push I needed. I left my secondary modern school in Midhurst and went instead to Portsmouth Technical College where my grandfather had taught.

To begin with I took English language and literature, geography and biology, but hated biology as it seemed to be all about cutting up animals and looking at what went on inside them, which was not what interested me at all. I switched to art and soon realised I had no natural talent, but practised all the time and was so proud when I finally passed. I really enjoyed my time at Tech College and it gave me a chance to grow up. More importantly, I now had four GCEs and could go back to Brinsbury. To my absolute delight, I was offered a place along with two other girls and nine boys. My dream of working with animals was one step closer to reality.

5

A Life's Work

Before starting my course at Brinsbury I faced some hard decisions about my animals. The course was residential and I would no longer be living at home to take care of them all. We agreed Sandy should remain with my mother who loved him. Biddy, a little grey rabbit, also stayed, but the other angora rabbits and my pony Prince were all to be sold. They were just too much for my mother who was still working full-time.

My formal training in animal husbandry really began at Brinsbury. There were dairy and beef herds, Hereford and Aberdeen Angus and I remember how the huge Hereford bull was so placid that we students could drive him. There were chickens and pigs to look after as well as arable farming. This was where I learned hoeing and scything, so useful to me later in keeping my garden and wood. Thinking back to those years in the mid-50s while lying immobile in bed, it was sometimes hard to believe I'd ever been so fit and strong.

After Brinsbury, I completed my training at Hampshire County Farm Institute near Winchester and then applied for my first job in St Ives in East Anglia with the Animal Health Trust Research Station, working with poultry. I got the job in spite of a rocky start to my interview when I gesticulated rather too wildly and sent an antique silver ink pot flying. Black ink spilt over the managing director's rather fine desk and across his papers. Somehow this failed to put him off. I was appointed Junior Research Assistant and the main part of my job was basically rearing chicks. I was very lucky, the job came with a small flat in the centre of town overlooking the river. While I was there, I sometimes looked after the manager's Border Collie, Nana, when he was away. I had a lovely time walking her to and from work along the riverbank. She was an intelligent dog but very sensitive to sound, especially worried by loud noises like thunder. I had to be very careful never to raise my voice to her.

The only downside to the happy time I spent there was an outbreak of fowl pest. All the birds in every shed at the station had to be slaughtered. Although we were sent home while they were dispatched, the job of cleaning up and disposing of their bodies fell to us on our return. The carnage was a horrendous sight. In my section most of the birds were just little chicks, only a few days old, which I had been carefully nurturing. Weeks of cleaning and disinfecting followed before we could restock, and the stench of burning carcasses was everywhere.

It was just after this time that I took a sailing holiday on the Norfolk Broads with a friend. I'd always loved boat holidays and this one reminded me of the many holidays I'd had there with my mother, brother and Sandy. When I returned to work I found a letter waiting for me from my mother with the sad news that Sandy had died. I knew how much she would miss having him around and remembered her commenting once how she thought she might like a Labrador at some point. This prompted me to do something I always advise people against. I went along to see a litter of yellow Labrador puppies and bought one for my mother for Christmas. The breeder offered me a cheaper price as the puppy had a small patch of white on his nose, meaning he could never be a show dog but he still cost me a whole week's wages.

The puppy was named Noel, appropriately enough. By this time my mother had given up the house in South Harting and resigned from the school where she had been teaching for thirty years as her own mother had died and she'd moved to a village just outside Bognor to look after her father. When I came home for the Christmas holiday she met me at Bognor station. Years later she told me that she still smiled at the memory of me arriving on the platform with a huge grin on my face, lugging a suitcase behind me and carrying a small puppy tucked under one arm. Noel was an instant hit with my mother who loved him dearly. Although I had tried with Sandy, this was really the first time I'd had the opportunity to train a dog from puppyhood and I enjoyed every minute of it. That summer I gave up my job in St Ives and moved to Felpham to stay with my mother. I walked Noel every day and, amongst other things, taught him to carry my beach towel for me. The holiday couldn't last for ever, though. As summer ended I knew it was time for me to look for a new job.

I wanted a change of scene and the chance of some adventure for a while. An advert in *Horse and Hound* for a job in Sweden sounded too good to be true. When I was offered it, I could hardly believe my luck. I'd been hired to live on a farm helping with the dogs and horses, plus sometimes looking after a four-year-old girl and baby boy. I wasn't too experienced with children but I liked the sound of the animals!

I flew out to Gothenburg and took a train to a local station where my new employer Brigitte met me in her Saab. It was already winter in Sweden and I vividly remember that first drive, whizzing along snow-packed roads through endless fir forests. We finally drew up at the farm, a beautiful weather-boarded house surrounded by gardens and outbuildings. I was met by Brigitte's two children: her little girl Tessa, who was blonde and very Swedish-looking, and Johan the baby, as well as Heinrich, her husband, who was a champion show jumper. Then I was led through the dining-room and along a passageway to my own suite of rooms which included the prettiest bedroom I had ever seen, with the bed standing in its own alcove. Despite the snow and freezing temperatures outside, it was warm and comfortable in the house. For the first time in my life I was discovering the joys of central heating and double glazing – quite a contrast to the way we lived in England in the early-60s.

In my free time, I would often take the dogs for a walk through the forests surrounding the farm. There was a German Pointer called Piccolo, the cowman's Elkhound, confusingly called Husky, who like his owner did not understand a word of English, and my favourite dog, Susie, a Miniature Dachshund. I had never really come across the breed before and was very impressed by the plucky little dog. She kept pace with the much larger Piccolo and Husky and even with a horse, running alongside Brigitte on her mare and me on a grey Welsh mountain pony called Melody. Susie was such a character, really adventurous and lively but perfectly happy to curl up on the sofa and be cuddled in the evenings.

We took long walks together along the forest tracks, often kept company by Amanda, a very large, tame pig I had trained to come when called, just like the dogs. I had worried I might have difficulty controlling Husky but found that if I used simple sign language instead of words, he could understand me perfectly. I've built on this experience and developed a range of hand signals which I've used with all my dogs since. It's especially useful when they're older and their hearing deteriorates, meaning they can still be active and have fun.

During my time with Brigitte's family, Susie had puppies. Brigitte was keen for me to take one back to England with me and I would have loved to, but the lengthy quarantine and strict regulations in place sadly made it impractical. I never forgot how lovely Susie had been, though. Many years later I finally acquired my own long-haired Miniature Dachshund, Eliza, who was with me for eighteen years.

I spent nine months in Sweden in total – my mother avoided mentioning the length of time in case anyone got the wrong idea! When I returned home, I couldn't believe how cold it felt. It was 1963, one of the century's coldest winters. The sea actually froze. I was happy to see my family again, though, and was delighted to find that Noel hadn't forgotten me at all or any of the things I had taught him. Next summer he was ready and waiting to carry my beach towel for me again.

I soon began a new job, researching broiler chickens for Buxted Chicken Company. As well as broadening my experience with poultry it was there that I really began to understand the training of dogs, something which would have an important influence on my future. Friends at the company owned a Golden Retriever called Judy. She had been trained by Mary and Mike to understand all sorts of commands. 'Judy, fire!' was enough to encourage her to move away from in front of the fire; 'Mat!' and she obediently stood on the mat with her dirty paws. Seeing what she was capable of opened my eyes to how much could be achieved with the right training.

When Judy had puppies, I was offered the pick of the litter. They were born on 14 March 1965 and to my delight

I saw them that first day. I soon found my puppy – or perhaps he found me. He was the biggest of the litter and there was already something about him that instantly appealed to me. He was inquisitive and lively but not overly so, seeming somehow self-contained yet alert. I also liked his colour which became a rich dark gold as he matured. I went away pondering names and decided on Crispin – all but one of my dog's names since have begun with the letter 'C'.

I was lucky to be able to visit him often over the next few weeks and finally took him home with me when he was eight weeks old. I was so excited and happy that day. It was a bumpy ride back in my black A35 and I kept glancing behind continually to check that my new puppy was fine. Crispin was always very calm and sensible, though, as Connie would be later at the same age. Home for me at that time was a caravan, very well equipped with electricity and a mini kitchen. It came with the job as I needed to be on site to check on the chickens late in the evening. Crispin settled in well there, sleeping in a bed under the table. I borrowed a book on dog training from the library and did lots with him.

He was with me all day at work, carrying my handbag for me and even collecting the wages from the director's office where he was well known. It was totally different owning a dog at that time – there were far fewer restrictions than today. He came with me to shops, banks, restaurants – anywhere I went, he went too. Being single, I did more socialising in those days and always took Crispin along with me. No other dog I have owned since has ever been as well socialised as, over the years, restrictions on dogs and where they are allowed to go have become so much tighter.

Attending dog club was also totally different in those

days. Absolutely no treats were offered, only very strict training using check chains, or choke chains as they were called, to control our dogs. Dogs were forced into different positions, rather than coaxed with kindness and treats. The dress code was also very different. I remember going for the first time wearing a smart dress and high-heeled shoes! People always dressed up in those days, but I had got it wrong with the heels. This was my introduction to competitive obedience and dog shows, and the thrill of working with a dog and being successful. Working on my own, I trained Crispin to do all sorts of interesting things, including carrying an egg in his mouth and even weeding the garden. I always tried to make it fun for him, though, rather than using the strict control that was normal for the day. I knew my methods made life enjoyable for Crispin and in the process produced a happy, confident dog that just loved to work.

I did make one huge mistake, though, that affected Crispin for life. He had displeased me one day – I can't even remember the details now apart from the fact that he was still quite a young dog. I was cross, and shouted at him and chased him into the caravan where he took refuge in his bed under the table. Being young and stupid, I crawled under the table and smacked him. He never forgot this, and for the rest of his life no one except me could lean over him when he was in his bed, which was strange as in some way he apparently did not connect me with his earlier experience.

It was also while I was at Buxted that I met my future husband. I had just broken up with a boyfriend and, although not very upset by the split, decided I needed a break and to try something completely different. I set off for a week's gliding course in Worcestershire. There I met a rather grumpy, disagreeable young man, a club member who worked the winch and tractor, and once, early in the week, managed to splatter me all over with mud. This was Fred, though by the end of the week I had amended my first impression of him. I had always imagined I would marry a fair-haired farmer whereas Fred was a dark-haired Londoner and an engineer. But we shared a love of the countryside and walking, and both adored water and boating. None of the blond farmers lasted the course, whereas nearly forty years later the dark-haired townie and I are still very happy.

As I lay in bed, reviewing my past and trying to plan what to do with Connie, it was the thought of everything I had formerly achieved which gave me hope. This wasn't, after all, the first time I'd been rendered immobile by pain, and the last time it had happened it was my Newfoundland Christie who had made all the difference. When I started having problems with my hips, finding it very hard to bend down and pick anything up it was Christie who came to my rescue.

She was a very big, strong dog who had been quite naughty and high-spirited as a youngster; it was my attempt to turn all this surplus energy in a useful direction which paid off for me later on. As a young dog Christie liked to tug on the washing hanging on the clothes line, and besides this used to bury her face in the washing basket I'd left on the lawn and run away with the socks. She also chewed the clothes pegs which I stored in a large bucket. I wanted to stop this antisocial behaviour so decided to play her at her own game. Taking the pegs off the clothes, I would throw them towards the peg bucket. When I missed, I began training Christie to find them for me and drop them back into the bucket. She loved this game and longed for me to miss, eagerly searching for the pegs in the grass.

Then, instead of letting her run away with socks, I decided she could pick them out of the basket and hand them straight to me, which she did successfully. As she was so strong, I soon found she could easily carry the empty washing basket back to the house; and, while I still carried the full clothes basket out to the line, she would happily carry the peg bucket for me. At first she would always tip out the pegs on to the grass, but before long the fun for her was in carrying the full bucket rather than emptying it.

I stepped up the level of training when she was five or six months old, which was when she accidentally knocked me over, breaking several ribs. We were out walking when the sky darkened ominously. Determined to get home before the storm broke, I called Christie who hurtled towards me enthusiastically. She simply failed to stop, bowling me over on to the ground where I lay, winded and in pain. As the broken ribs I'd suffered made it impossible for me to bend over and pick anything up after that, I decided to teach Christie to do it for me, especially as she was responsible for my injuries in the first place.

Unfortunately, my hips really deteriorated during the twelve years Christie was with me so, gradually, she took on the role of my assistance dog, helping me to walk when I became unsteady and with getting up from chairs when this became difficult. She learned to do an incredible number of useful tasks in the house and garden, and on walks it was reassuring to know I could rely on her to help me up and down steep slopes. It was this previous experience with Christie that really gave me the idea of teaching Connie to be my personal assistant and home help.

6

A Happy Reunion

It was early-morning and the cottage was still and silent. I lay in bed enjoying the peace and listened as the lesser spotted woodpecker began his hammering on one of the old oak posts supporting the porch. Far away across the valley I could just hear an answering call from another woodpecker. I thought about the day ahead with some apprehension. Fred was going to collect Connie from the boarding kennels and bring her home. I was longing to see her and very excited, but also rather worried. I shifted position in bed, slowly and carefully, trying not to make the back pain worse. I was barely mobile, how would I cope with looking after my little puppy again? Puppy?

Then I realised with a jolt that of course Connie would no longer be a baby. She had gone away to kennels on 26 January. It was now 6 April. Ten weeks had passed and Connie was an incredible seven months old. It was a shock to realise how much she would have grown. Would she even remember me after so long? She had gone away at such an important time in her development, but there was no point in reproaching myself for that. For now I would just look forward to seeing her again.

Later that morning I heard the sound of our car pulling up outside the cottage. I carefully manoeuvred myself out of bed and, with the help of my walking stick, propped myself against the wall for support in case Connie knocked into me. I had the soft little bed she used to sleep on in my free hand, ready to give her. She used to love to carry this around before she went away. My heart was beating fast as Fred opened the door and Connie rushed in, seeming delighted to see me. She immediately took hold of her old bed, twirling round and round in excitement, her tail wagging frantically. I took my opportunity to study the changes in her. She was definitely much bigger, I noticed her legs were longer too, but she still had her soft, slightly fluffy baby coat. I was also thrilled to see how fit she looked – in total contrast to me!

She soon quietened down and came over to me for a huge fuss. I needn't have worried, she hadn't forgotten me at all. 'Who's a good girl? Who's the most beautiful dog in the world?' I murmured softly. She responded to my silly dog talk by gazing adoringly at me, pressing herself carefully against me as if she understood just how fragile I was. I was quite overwhelmed by emotion as I looked down into her funny little face and gentle, expressive eyes.

Greetings over, Connie wanted to investigate and immediately checked out my sleeping arrangements. I was once again back in the spare bedroom-cum-office that I had used when she first arrived as it was simply impossible for me to get upstairs. I liked being there as I was near the kitchen and didn't feel so cut off from the rest of the house. Connie had always been a very inquisitive puppy and was soon busily sniffing around the room: bedclothes, library books, pile of underwear and reading glasses, all seemed to meet with her approval. Then she spied my shoes. I wondered if she would remember our game after so long.

'Pick up,' I said, brightly and expectantly. She glanced back at me as if to say, Don't worry, I know what to do, then pounced happily on to the nearest shoe, brought it to me and rushed off to retrieve the next one. After that she sat perfectly, waiting for her treat. Luckily I had one to hand. This was brilliant. It was as if she had never been away.

After she'd finished pottering in the garden, checking out all her old haunts, it was time for her dinner. I struggled slowly to the kitchen, determined to manage this simple task by myself. It took longer than usual but I filled her food bowl. Connie immediately ran to the place where she had always been fed and sat waiting politely. She had definitely not forgotten her manners, but would she remember that I had taught her to bring back her bowl to the sink when she had finished? To my absolute delight she immediately brought the empty bowl to me. She looked as pleased as I felt, her tail held up straight and proud. She quickly gave me the bowl, knowing she would then receive a few more pieces of dinner. I should point out here that I reserve a small amount of her daily food ration to use for rewards, rather than giving her too much extra food.

It had been an exciting but tiring day and by now I was exhausted. After checking that there was a toy box ready for Connie in my bedroom, I went through the difficult business of trying to lower myself into bed without sending my back into spasms of agony. It was time to take my next assortment of pills and potions, and my body was letting me know it. Finally I lay down, sighing with relief as my head rested on the pillow. Connie rushed in then, obviously wondering where I'd got to. There you are, I could see her thinking as she discovered my hiding place beneath the duvet. What are you doing there? her puzzled expression seemed to ask as she thrust her cold wet nose into my face. I had to smile. She obviously thought it was great fun, having my face on the same level as her own.

Sure of my whereabouts now, Connie wandered away for another tour of the room and soon found the toy box I had left out for her. Tail wagging, she delightedly rummaged around until she discovered her favourite little yellow ball and at once brought it to me hopefully, wanting a game. From my awkward position, lying on my side, I managed a very feeble throw. Luckily the ball rolled under a chair which made retrieving it far more tricky and the game more interesting. Connie quickly grasped the idea that if she brought me a toy, even though I was lying down in bed, she could still have her game. This was another small success, and such a relief for me. I felt happier and more hopeful than I had for weeks.

That first night after Connie's return I dozed fitfully, checking the clock frequently to see if it was time to take more painkillers. It was barely light before I was fully awake again, lying perfectly still, knowing from bitter experience that the slightest movement would trigger pain. I heard the dawn chorus starting with the first muted songs, gradually building into a wonderful crescendo of sound. Connie slept on soundly in her puppy pen. I was amazed to see how happily and easily she had settled back into her old routine. I was also surprised by how small her puppy pen now looked, remembering how big it had appeared on her first day here.

Waiting for Connie and the rest of the house to waken, I ran through my plan of action again in my head. She had such a wonderful temperament: very laid-back and sensible, but at the same time bright, intelligent and very curious, which was the perfect combination. It was always vitally important to me that Connie should enjoy life and have plenty of mental as well as physical stimulation, no matter what my own physical state happened to be.

My primary idea was to teach her to be my personal

assistant in the home and garden. That sounded very optimistic, I knew, but no one could be in any doubt how much I needed one at that moment. Helping me would keep her occupied, and I was also sure I could make it fun for her. From my point of view, it was a challenging project and the best incentive I had to get fit again as soon as possible.

I had decided that I would also continue with her obedience and show-ring training, as far as I could from home since obviously it was impossible for me to go to any dog clubs in my present state. This aspect of Connie's education was an important part of my plan as it would provide greater variety for her, which I have always considered essential for dogs. Even with my present extremely limited mobility, I was hopeful we would be able to go to dog shows later in the year. Meanwhile obedience training would provide the first building blocks for her dog assistance work. Before we could progress to more complicated work, I had to make sure that Connie understood all the simple obedience commands, such as 'Come', 'Sit', 'Down', 'Fetch', and 'Give'. These were just the beginning as she would also need to learn to watch me, following my hand signals and body language, and listen carefully to my voice and instructions.

Over the years, I had done a great deal of the early training with my dogs just using the kitchen and utility room, the doorways and even our small hall. My dogs had all learnt the initial stages of a range of activities there, including obedience work, pulling a sledge and even a boat. Later they had progressed to more advanced work outside. Although at that time I couldn't even sit in a car, let alone drive, I was lucky enough to have a variety of locations close to hand on our own land which I could use for Connie's work, play and exercise.

It had been a real struggle to buy the adjacent wood and fields shortly after we'd moved into the cottage. But although it had meant we were without carpets and furniture in parts of the house, we'd never regretted the hardship and the whole family had enjoyed the extra space and freedom we'd gained. We have gardens surrounding the house, two small fields, and roughly an acre of woodland including some steeper land leading down to a small stream. There is also the woodland pond where I planned to take Connie later on, to practise her water work. I had no doubt that she would love it as much as my previous Newfoundlands had.

Cassie in particular had been an excellent swimmer. She had not been with me very long when, without warning, she jumped into a neighbour's flooded stream, and to my alarm was swept away in the strong current. I needn't have worried. She emerged on the bank, a little downstream, unscathed and having thoroughly enjoyed the experience! Not surprisingly, she went on to do a great deal of water work and competed in the Newfoundland Water Trials. Both Cassie and Christie loved pulling boats in the water, especially if one of the children was on board and needed 'rescuing'.

The wood was not large but contained so many different areas and types of habitat for wildlife that I knew Connie would always be able to find something interesting there. Over the years the wood has become my special place. It's where I go to sit quietly and think, to watch the passing seasons or hide away to watch the wildlife in secret. I love clearing the brambles from around the pond in early-summer, and checking the stream is flowing freely with no build up of rocks or silt in winter. I have my own particular places to sit – rough benches or sometimes just a convenient fallen tree trunk. When I was laid up in bed, it was *the* place I longed to go to, in my mind climbing up through my wood over the style and to the top of the hill.

As I lay thinking about her training, absent-mindedly I started to stretch, and gasped with shock as a jolt of pain shot through my back. What a ridiculous optimist I was. Just working out how to stagger out of bed, let alone walk anywhere, made my plans of a few minutes ago seem a touch ambitious. I checked the clock, relieved to see it was time for my next round of painkillers. It was good timing. Connie was stirring now and would soon be up and about, full of energy, ready to start her day. I was determined that once the pills began their numbing work I would make it to the field, to play with her there and begin her training in earnest.

7

Fun and Games

With the help of my stick, I did indeed make it through the garden to our field that first morning, albeit with gritted teeth and by mustering all my willpower. But this was an important breakthrough for me and such a wonderful boost to my confidence. Connie seemed not to notice the slowness of our progress and was again so careful of me I was convinced she understood my fragile condition.

I'd decided this first lesson in our new training regime would be tracking. Armed with an inviting fake-fur glove, I walked a few paces and then dropped it. 'Seek, seek,' I said in an excited voice, at the same time encouraging her to sniff my hand which still had the scent of the glove on it. Anyone watching would have wondered what on earth I was doing as I bent over as far as I was able to pretend to sniff the ground then walked back towards the glove. Connie looked at me inquisitively, obviously curious about this odd new game. I sniffed loudly and pointed to the ground again, repeating the command, 'Seek, seek.' At that point she began snuffling her way through the grass until she found the glove, which at this early stage in training was clearly visible.

'Good girl! What a clever dog,' I encouraged her as she rushed back to show me what she had found. She gave up the glove easily in return for a treat and I followed this with a game of tossing the glove into nearby long grass for her to find. Enjoying the game, Connie couldn't wait to try again and we repeated the whole seek and find exercise a couple more times. As Connie progressed and became more proficient, I developed the game further until I could drop the glove anywhere in our field, knowing she would still be able to find it. Later still I expanded the search area to include our wood and even the big field on the far side of it. I would very slowly walk as far as I could then send Connie back to find the glove, or perhaps her dog lead or an old sock, which challenged her and at the same time gave her masses of exercise. Eventually, she would gallop way out of sight to find anything I'd dropped, but on that first morning I was more than satisfied with our few successful finds of the glove. I'd first practised tracking with Crispin many years ago before I was married. He would seek an old glove and tear back to me, so excited at his own cleverness that often there would be nothing left to take from him but a few scraps as he had swallowed the rest en route.

Another crafty game of mine from these early days with Connie was to take two squeaky toys into the field and surreptitiously throw one over the hedge and back into the garden. To retrieve it, Connie had to run along one side of the hedge, through the gate into the garden then back along the hedge on the other side. I encouraged her all the time by madly squeaking the second toy. This game had the advantage of giving Connie the maximum amount of exercise from minimal input by me. All I had to do was stand in the field, propped on my stick. There was extra excitement for Connie if she could not see where the toy had landed in the garden and needed to sniff it out. I also taught her a new command for this game, calling 'Go round!' encouragingly while waving my arm in the right direction, until she set off.

From the start, Connie's progress was fast and mine rather slow. I had to be very careful as I was easily over-tired. Whenever I felt frustrated, I tried to fix on how much better I was; how a few short weeks before, lying immobile in bed with no dog, I would have been delighted just to be able to hobble outside, let alone make it all the way to the field with my adorable Connie by my side, brightening my mood.

There was no doubting, though, that Connie needed more exercise than I could provide her with, and it was also important that she should get used to socialising with other people and other dogs. As I was a little stronger, I felt up to seeing visitors again. I would lie in bed holding court with friends and relations, sipping sherry or tea as if this was all perfectly normal. Connie loved the extra people and attention.

When my back problem first began, I had cancelled a lunch date with Mary, one of my oldest friends. Shortly after Connie's return we eventually caught up on each other's news over our postponed lunch, though at my home and with Mary supplying the food. Stella also came to stay, bringing Trampus, her elderly Welsh Springer Spaniel, with her. Trampus was always so perfectly groomed, with his rich red and white coat gleaming, and knew exactly how to behave as befitted his mature status. Connie was delighted to have a new playmate and he was happy to play along, but would sternly reprimand the younger puppy if she overstepped the mark. Needless to say, Connie quickly learned to be careful and respectful.

Before Connie went away to kennels, she had met another young dog, Oliver, a clever black Labrador. He belonged to my good friend Sas, and was just a few months older than Connie. They had instantly liked one another in those first weeks and were delighted to meet up again. The pair were very well matched in size and exuberance, and in their enthusiasm for wild, exciting games. They loved nothing better than to tear away around the field, chasing each other madly, rolling over and over. Other times they would dash into the wood, plunging in and out of the pond. During these mad moments I kept well out of the way, terrified of injury. I'm afraid I allowed Sas to run the risk of broken bones after being accidentally charged by our wild dogs.

Another good friend, Jo, appeared regularly to take Connie for long outings along the local lanes and tracks, walking her on the lead and giving her vital exercise. There were occasions, when Connie was first back with me, when it was as much as I could manage to stumble into the hall and hand her over before gratefully sinking back into bed. Connie absolutely adored Jo and still gives her a special welcome. I know she has never forgotten all those early walks and that there is a special bond between them. I liked to think of it as a fond aunt indulging a favoured niece, especially as Jo often spoilt Connie with all her favourite treats.

It was not ideal that I couldn't provide all the exercise Connie needed, but we were more than managing and at least I knew my growing puppy was happy. I took my own sense of frustration to be a sign that my condition was improving. At first I could concentrate only on making it from one dose of medication to the next. Now I had my life at home back and longed only to be fit enough to enjoy my woodland walks once more.

It was during one of Connie's walks with Jo, on my slow trek back to bed, that I glanced towards the French windows. Close by the patio steps, half a dozen deer stood quietly grazing our lawn. They appeared relaxed and totally unconcerned at being so close to the cottage. I could clearly see every detail of them, even their tiny budding antlers. Some cropped the lush April grass while others busily trimmed the hedges. In the past I would not have been too pleased as deer had often damaged my roses and other prize shrubs, but on this occasion all was forgiven. It was as if they had miraculously appeared in answer to my longing to see more of my beloved countryside and wildlife. I enjoyed watching them until they grew bored with the lawn. First one then another gracefully jumped the hedge in orderly fashion. They slipped away in single file into the wood, vanishing silently between the trees.

In early-June I had just returned with Connie from a successful training session in the field when I heard the woodpecker calling to her young. She had obviously found a mate. I thought with satisfaction how far both Connie and I had come since that morning in early-April when I'd listened to the woodpecker's hammering and wondered if I could cope.

I kept looking out of the window and eventually saw a young woodpecker hiding in the huge field maple. It was peeping around a branch, obviously waiting for Mum to bring a piece of nut from the feeder by the porch. Baby woodpeckers always remind me of little schoolboys wearing bright red school caps. One year I watched four of them perched in a line on an old apple tree. For some reason they had displeased their parent who smacked each one smartly on its red head whereupon they ducked down, looking guilty. As they grow bigger the mother teaches her young to eat direct from the bird feeder. They are quite shy birds and always hide behind the post. They bravely hang on to the nutfeeder, frantically flapping their wings, but often fall off with much undignified fluttering before they finally get the hang of it. The adults can manage perfectly, supporting themselves with their stiff tails tucked under the feeder.

As the weeks passed I continued Connie's work indoors as well as fun and games outside. I was lucky for a few weeks as the weather stayed dry with bright frosty mornings, which meant Connie's fur remained quite clean. Her coat was still fairly short as she had not yet developed her more profuse adult fur. But I always knew that grooming and drying would be a challenge for me. Although I was stronger by now, bending was still extremely difficult. Of course, the day came when the weather changed and Connie was soaking wet. Inspiration struck me. I laid several old towels in her pen, threw in a large bone and shut the door with Connie inside. She settled happily with the bone, rolling about chewing it, thoroughly enjoying herself. And, a blessing for me, very effectively drying herself at the same time.

My next project was to teach Connie to fetch her own bowl and, more importantly, food. This involved her taking her bowl from the cupboard to hand to me, then carrying her little yellow beach bucket to the pantry where I would fill it with food for her to cart back to the sink. I would then fill the bowl ready for her to eat.

As with all our exercises, this was broken down into simple stages. The first step was easy. I would kick the bowl to make it rattle and attract Connie's attention to it, stored away on a low shelf. She was already used to picking it up after dinner. The next stage was more difficult as she did not like holding the bucket's handle. I worked on this as a completely separate exercise, with lots of treats after one short hold. I never force a dog to hold or carry anything; they must want to do it. Connie soon got the idea and happily carried the bucket to the pantry where I would offer her a reward. I then had the tricky task of encouraging her to carry a bucket full of food that she naturally wanted to eat. At first I placed just three tiny pieces at the bottom of the bucket, at the same time showing her a particularly succulent piece of chicken held in my hand. 'Hold,' I said, handing her the bucket while making sure she was focused on the tempting treat I was holding rather than the food in the bucket. It worked. She carried the bucket to the sink where I immediately offered her the chicken. Over a period of time I gradually put more food into the bucket until before long she was carrying a bucketful, always with the promise of an extra tasty treat. This became our party trick for a time as visitors were always amazed to see a dog carrying her own food.

In the wild, wolves hunt and work to find food. I think it is good for dogs, who are after all descended from wolves, sometimes to work a little for theirs too. With this in mind I still occasionally scatter some of Connie's breakfast outside on the patio or in the grass, so that she has to hunt around to find it all. This helps her scent work and keeps her happily occupied for quite a while. I have also always been keen to avoid the sort of situation where a dog feels it must guard its food. Dogs often become over-protective which can lead to accidents, especially with young children. My aim has always been to build up trust, but also to make sure my dogs respect our food and will not snatch it. Connie has a hollow bone and from the first I trained her to bring it to me, to stuff with cheese or some other titbit that she loves. As a result she happily gives me her bone, knowing that it will have more cheese inside when I return it to her. She still loves me to hold her chew stick, too, just as she did when I first had her.

When we are eating Connie knows she will not be given

anything from the table and curls up well away from us. As soon as we have finished and are clearing the dishes, she sits beside the dishwasher knowing that I might have a treat for her then. From the start I kept the kitchen worktop clear, especially if I had to leave the room for a moment. Food within sight and reach is just too much of a temptation for most dogs.

Another common problem is the family dog raiding the rubbish bin. My solution is probably unconventional but it works for me. As soon as Connie was tall enough, she learned to deposit rubbish into the bin rather than take it out. By that time she had learned the word 'Drop', which means she should drop the item where I say rather than giving it to me. 'Rubbish bin,' I would shout as I dropped something on to the floor and opened the bin lid. Connie's eyes would gleam with anticipation as she let the rubbish fall into the bin, knowing that a tasty reward would quickly follow.

She was learning fast, although things didn't always go to plan. I was very proud of how good she was at picking up all sorts of things from the floor and handing them to me. I tried a variety of textures – hard, squashy, crunchy, crinkly – anything, in fact, that was safe. I boasted of her cleverness to an early visitor and demonstrated it by dropping a pen for her to pick up. Connie answered my command but proceeded to crunch the pen up noisily. I think I muttered the excuse that it must have been cracked, but shortly after this I realised how important it was also to teach her the word 'Leave'. I accidentally dropped a knife and as Connie rushed forward to retrieve it for me, I was terrified she would cut herself. I was so worried that I reacted in completely the wrong way. As a result Connie thought this a great game, rushing dangerously about the kitchen, brandishing the knife like some demented canine pirate. Luckily, she came to no harm, while I learned a lesson on the importance of remaining calm and, more practically, concentrated on teaching her the word 'Leave' alongside 'Pick up'.

This simple lesson was invaluable just a few days later when I dropped one of the twenty-five pills I was taking daily for my back. It rolled away and I couldn't find it anywhere. I was worried that Connie would swallow it. In the end, I asked her to search for it while I kept a watchful eye on her. After a circuit of the room she lay flat in front of a pine blanket chest, staring beneath it. Sure enough, when I did eventually manage to bend down and look, there was the missing pill.

Connie quickly learned to bring me my socks and shoes, and within a couple of months was also having fun pulling off my socks without biting my toes as well as removing slip-on shoes and sandals. I thought it would be useful to teach her to pick up my walking stick if I dropped it, and it was interesting to see that from the first she always gave me the handle rather than the dirty end, probably because that was the part with more of my scent on it.

Whatever I am doing, I talk to my dog constantly. Whether I am out or just quietly at home with Connie, I am always talking to her: giving her commands, praising her and generally encouraging her.

And so the spring passed with Connie's training progressing well as she quickly mastered new skills. I too was slowly feeling stronger but still needed to take care and rest often. In the afternoons when I lay down on my bed in the downstairs office I needed only to say, 'Rug, Connie,' and my wonderful nurse would immediately fetch a blanket to cover me. It reminded me so much of the caring Nana in the nursery in *Peter Pan*. By early-May the sun was hot enough for me to relax outside on a lounger next to the ancient summer house in our field. This seemed like real luxury, especially as Connie, ever useful, carried my cushion for me. For some reason, that May the field was covered with dandelions. At one point it was a sea of round seed heads gently waving in the breeze. Everything was new to Connie that year. Intrigued by the sight, she playfully jumped and pounced on each one until she was almost hidden by a cloud of drifting seeds. A few days later she tried to do the same with bumble bees, with rather less success. I quickly rescued the unfortunate few she managed to catch and began teaching her to leave well alone.

I have always enjoyed a challenge and like to set myself targets and projects. Ever the optimist, I had entered Connie for her first dog show just after she came home from kennels. It was at the end of May and I had been absolutely convinced I would be fit enough to handle her by then. But with the show just a few weeks away, it was obvious even to me that I would not. This was a breed show where the dog must first stand to be examined by the judge, then go round the ring with its handler at a smart pace for its movement to be assessed. You have to run for that part which was simply impossible for me. As Connie had not been back to ring-craft classes, I also had no idea how she would behave at a busy show among lots of other dogs and people. Very disappointed, I had decided to cancel when Stella, my very own fairy godmother, made it all possible. She generously offered to drive us there which meant her getting up before the crack of dawn as she lives some fifty miles away and, more reluctantly, she even agreed to take Connie into the ring for me.

This of course meant Connie and I needed to practise for the show ring. We covered 'Stand' with her remaining rock steady, head up and paws neatly placed, while I showed her some tasty treat. We also tried 'Walk on', the command for her to run round the ring. I rather pathetically speeded up my stumbling pace to give her the general idea and Connie, her usual sweet-tempered self, happily took part in this latest game I'd devised for her.

Stella arrived early on the day of the show and we set off with an unusually clean and tidy Newfoundland. Most dogs love shows and Connie was no exception. Taking one look at the mass of excited dogs and keen exhibitors, Stella immediately took Connie's lead, just in time, as she merrily lunged forward hoping for a game with all these friendly strangers. I tried not to cringe as she jumped up to make friends with as many people as possible. After her first burst of wild enthusiasm, Connie calmed down and Stella quickly had her under control. It was soon time for the puppy class and Stella reluctantly agreed to take Connie into the ring for me.

'I don't do feet,' she grumbled good-humouredly as I carefully explained how to place Connie's paws correctly so that she would stand properly for the judge. 'I'll be no good at this,' Stella warned. 'Obedience, yes, I can do that, no problem, but a breed class . . . ? Well, I'll just do my best.' She is in fact brilliant with dogs and they always behave wonderfully well for her.

As it turned out, neither Stella nor I had any reason to be concerned. I was surprised by how well Connie behaved, especially with other puppies running round. I held my breath as she stood for the judge but needn't have worried. She stayed steady and made no attempt to jump up. There was no award for her that time but it was a good first show, with dog and handler performing very well.

The day brought back happy memories for me of other shows with different dogs. Cassie, my first Newfoundland, was a lovely show dog and did well at championship shows where she even gained a challenge certificate – dogs need to win three to be a champion. She also qualified for Crufts and was shown there.

I would go to dog shows, taking the children wth me. David would be looked after by Barry and Michael who were only about eight or nine. When David was still quite small he could often be found curled up, sleeping soundly on one of the dog benches. It would be frowned on today.

I started going to shows with Christie when she was six months old and her behaviour was very different from Connie's. At the refreshment stalls she would lunge forward, sending anything on the counters flying and scattering other customers in her wake. Always a friendly dog, there seemed little hope of her standing still for the judges as she leaped up to offer them a greeting. She eventually calmed down and before long behaved very well, although she never forgot a bad fright she suffered at one of her first shows. A bench collapsed beneath her and, although she was usually such a brave, strong dog, she steadfastly refused to go anywhere near the benches after that.

I have to admit, dog shows are the only times I break my strict food rules. I always share my picnic lunch with my canine companions as a special treat.

8

Connie's First Summer

Connie's first dog show marked a milestone in our joint progress. Everything seemed just a little easier after it. By early-June I was walking in the lane again. Moving was still difficult but each day I went a little further. At last I could enjoy different views of the countryside as it blossomed into summer. I paused to rest and watch the great tits frantically feeding their babies in a gnarled cherry tree or the heron with its lazily flapping wings, looking strangely prehistoric as it flew towards the nearby lake.

Connie was proving to be very good at walking on a loose lead. I've always practised lead and heelwork in the lanes around our cottage. They're usually very peaceful and quiet, with hardly a car or another person about, and are relatively confined which can be useful. Lots of otherwise well-behaved dogs pull on the lead and my usual system is to encourage them to walk to heel for three paces then let them loose on a long lead after which I call them back to heel. It's really about teaching the dog that it is worth walking well to heel without pulling because they will always be rewarded afterwards with a loose lead. Connie was quick to catch on and I always carried an interesting squeaky toy to keep her attention focussed on me. She knew she would be able to explore the fascinating scents on the grass verges and would always be rewarded with a game at the end. I've always tried to vary the pace and routes I take, though this was more difficult for me during my back problem.

There was just one exception to Connie's good behaviour. On the rare occasions we saw someone else out walking with a dog, she would lurch forward enthusiastically at top speed. Because I was so fragile on those early walks I did not dare to hang on, for fear of injury, and so let her go. Unfortunately, this became a bad habit of hers which is still proving hard to break. Sometimes, however knowledgeable you are and whatever you try, you just need a little extra something to help you solve a problem. Christie, for instance, was always quite a dominant dog, and although she was never bad-tempered or nasty in any way, around the age of five to six months she really tried to test me. This is a common age for this type of behaviour to start, it probably equates to the stroppy teenage years in humans and can occur at different times in dogs between the ages of six and eighteen months. Christie was always trying to grab her lead and because she was so strong could really drag me along. I spent ages trying to cure her with all my usual tricks with toys and treats, but to my frustration nothing seemed to work. She would start well but invariably begin pulling and dragging me when we turned for home. Finally one day the sky had turned ominously dark and we were heading back. Christie had begun her usual pulling. At the exact same second as I sternly commanded, 'Leave!' a giant clap of thunder rumbled overhead. Christie started in surprise and stopped pulling. She never did it again. I am now waiting for that little extra touch of magic to cure Connie, though as running to greet other dogs seems to be her only fault, I know I am very lucky.

When I was able to make it as far as the end of the lane, Connie liked the important job of carrying the post for me in her own little red handbag. Many people teach their dog to fetch but few teach 'Carry'. I've found this useful in so many different ways. All my dogs, from Crispin with the wages, to Connie today, have always really enjoyed it. Over the years I've found the easiest way to teach this is to give your dog something to carry when on the lead while you run, or walk briskly, about level with the dog's hind quarters, all the time making encouraging comments. Because they are slightly in front of you the dog keeps going, holding the bag, cushion or whatever carefully. We have on occasion met another dog while Connie is carrying her red handbag and sometimes they look at her rather quizzically. Maybe it's my imagination but she seems to hold the bag just a little higher and more proudly when this happens.

We had a rather embarrassing incident recently as a result of her one bad habit. Connie happened to be carrying her bag to the post and we had just passed a neighbour's driveway when Connie suddenly took off, jerking the lead from my hand and haring away down the drive. I could just glimpse flashes of black dog and red handbag vanishing fast. I realised she must have caught sight of the dog who lives there, one she particularly likes. The weather had been rainy and we had been walking for a while. Connie was muddy and wet. I trailed behind feeling rather cross and could just see her through the trees, heading for the house.

As I watched she veered away on a diversion to examine the river running through the garden, dropping her bag, and my post, on the boggy bank dangerously close to the water's edge. She then galloped across the lawn to the house where she could see her Collie friend behind a fence barking excitedly. Connie rushed up to greet him. Our neighbour, hearing the commotion, opened the front door wide. I shouted a warning, but too late. A dirty, dishevelled Connie, thinking this escapade great fun, raced through the doorway and into the immaculate house beyond. 'Connie! *Connie*! Come out!' shouted my poor neighbour. I stood there, also wet and muddy, and with a sinking heart remembered the pristine cream carpet in their sitting-room. With my dog finally subdued and on a short lead, clasped firmly by my side, I then had to slink off across the expanse of lawn to the riverbank, to retrieve the handbag containing my post before it was swept away.

That first summer saw me resuming more of my usual activities. I found that if I was very careful I could manage a little gardening which is something I love to do. Connie as always, stayed close beside me, keen to be helpful. She quickly learned to pick up small tools when asked and to pass them to me, or to drop flowerpots into the wheel-barrow. One of her favourite jobs was to carry the washing-up bowl I found so useful to load the weeds into while I gingerly crawled between the flowerbeds. She would also, if instructed, help pull up the weeds, something I taught Crispin to do over thirty years before.

I also use gardening as an opportunity to practise Connie's scent work. I am constantly 'losing' my gardening gloves, sometimes even over the hedge in the next field. She obligingly rushes away to find them, probably wondering how I manage to drop them so regularly. Scent work is such fun for dogs and something that comes naturally, especially to working breeds. My Miniature Dachshund Eliza had such a good nose for tracking that I could always rely on her to find our way home from anywhere. I remember getting completely lost once staying with my aunt and uncle in Bournemouth, and although the surroundings were totally unfamiliar Eliza soon had us back on the right track. After the hurricane in October 1987 the devastation was so great, with so many trees and other landmarks down, that it was impossible to keep your bearings, even in our own wood which I always thought I knew so well. But Eliza always knew exactly where she was. Her little nose would go down and she would snuffle intently about until she found the right scent, and then set off, sure-footed and confident. She never let me down and I loved to watch her work.

In July I began driving again which meant I could do my own shopping after months of home deliveries. It was ridiculously exciting to be able to walk along the super-market aisles myself and choose what I wanted. This was another opportunity for Connie to act as my willing assist-ant. She helped bring in the shopping. At first she just carried it from the utility room to the kitchen, but later she proudly took a big basket to the car for me to fill with shopping which she then carefully carried back to the house. Occa-sionally she was so excited about her task she would rush around the garden holding the basket, taking a crafty crunch at the handle as she went. This was quickly cured by making sure there were two treats ready and waiting for her, one in the car and one in the kitchen, so she could not wait to take her basket from one place to the other.

Connie made herself more useful each day, fetching, carrying and picking up anything I wanted. She had learned to drop dirty washing into the laundry basket and also to take things out of the washing machine and tumble dryer; she even liked to pick up the detergent ball from the cup-board for me. When I was able to bath again I would often bring my underwear downstairs for Connie to put in the laundry basket. This was invariably just before her dinner time so she could hardly wait to complete this job knowing she would be fed immediately afterwards. Occasionally I would change my routine, to be met with a look of disgust from Connie when I came downstairs empty handed. 'What no knickers? Surely you're not wearing the dirty ones again!' her expression seemed to say.

I was managing to walk further each day and could now confidently make it into our wood. Connie still loved to play Hide and Seek as she had when still a very young puppy and this helped develop her scent work alongside her ability to watch and follow me. I had a ball on a rope which made throwing easier for me and would hurl this across the stream. It gave Connie a satisfying romp as she had to run down the gully, leap across the stream and race back up the slope carrying the ball ready for me to throw again. It came as something of a shock to realise when I stopped to rest in the shade one day, on my railway-sleeper bench, that Connie and I were now busy every day. My months of constant bed rest were well and truly behind me. As if to prove this point, the next day we drove to the seaside to see Derek, Stella and Trampus. This time Connie boldly ventured into the waves, splashing in and out of the water, romping on the beach with other dogs and generally loving her day out.

There was also a visit to our youngest son David's new flat in Guildford which I had not yet seen. When we arrived, David showed us into the tiny hall. 'My flat's on the first floor,' he said, leading the way upstairs.

Fred and I followed but Connie stopped dead at the bottom step. 'Come on Connie,' I called. 'Come see David.' I was confident she would come as she is always so obedient. But Connie wasn't to be moved. She dug in her toes and stared suspiciously at the stairs. David came back down to make a big fuss of her before going back upstairs, calling encouragingly. Connie loves David so I was sure she would follow him but she resolutely refused to budge.

In the end we left her behind in the hall where she was quite safe and carried on up to David's flat. I still thought she would follow after a minute or two but while we admired the flat and drank coffee, Connie still remained downstairs. She had obviously decided that stairs were very dangerous and should never be climbed by any sane dog. She spent the entire visit curled up asleep in the hall which was hardly any bigger than she was, content to know we were close by. Of course I knew it was my fault as I had taught her too well that she was never allowed upstairs at home. At the time it did not seem to be too much of a problem.

Feeling stronger and more confident by the day, I braved another open breed show, this time on my own. I held Connie with one hand and pulled the trolley containing our gear in the other, all the way from the car park to the showground. I still could not run round the ring with her but an old friend there offered to do it for me while I managed the showing part, which is allowed but not ideal. We came fourth out of four, but Connie behaved so perfectly that I didn't mind at all. Just the fact that I could be there was a small triumph for me. I followed this up at the dog show at a local country fair. These are the types of show which I really enjoy because they are such fun for the dogs, there's just so much going on. Connie was very excited by all the activity – there were horses, traction engines belching steam and tooting their whistles, busy stalls, billowing flags and lots of children making a fuss of her. I've noticed all my Newfoundlands have attracted attention, partly because they are still not very common as a breed and people are always interested to know more. Connie loved the attention and was very happy to let even the little toddlers stroke her fur – I just had to be careful that she didn't sneak a crafty lick of one of their ice creams.

As we left behind the general fair and made for the dog show, Connie suddenly became wildly excited. I soon realised why as I spotted Sas with Connie's favourite dog friend, Oliver, among the mêlée of people and dogs. There was a confusion of plunging dogs and tangled leads as the two friends eagerly greeted one another. The pair of them had a few mad moments but quickly settled down and Connie and I were soon in the ring for the Working Puppy class. For the first time, I did everything myself, including the running. I was pleased about that, though the judge later commented that I should perhaps get someone else to handle Connie for me. I was obviously letting down her performance. Still, he couldn't know what an improvement I'd made and I was thrilled to see how well Connie coped with all the noise and distractions when she was used to such a quiet life.

Mid-August brought another companion dog show and fête and was to be an auspicious day for us both. It was a perfect sunny summer's day. Connie was brushed without a tangle or bramble in sight, ready for the show in the next village. The playing field where it was held was buzzing with activity. Connie was fascinated by it all, though I think she was rather shocked by the plate-smashing and the over-enthusiastic band. We threaded our way through the crowds, jostling at the plant stall and queuing at the refreshment tent en route. The dog show was being held under the shade of some trees nearby. This time Connie was entered for the puppy class, which is for any breed or sex. This is quite a tricky category as some breeds mature faster than others, giving them the advantage, which is particularly true of certain small breeds.

Once we were in the ring Connie was again very well behaved, and I managed a slightly better run this time. In the tense moments when you position your dog to stand for the judge, I'm afraid I rather smugly noted some of the other puppies who were jumping about and dragging their owners around the ring. I was still surprised to be among those called into the centre of the ring. The judge lined us all up and, to my utter amazement, I was then presented with a large red rosette. We had won first prize! It was just a small show but at that moment I could not have been more pleased if it had been Crufts. In an instant I remembered the first rosette I'd ever won at a show like this. It was over forty years ago with Crispin, who was also awarded Best in Show.

Afterwards Connie and I headed for the trees to enjoy our picnic lunch and bask in our triumph. How far we had both come from that morning in early-April when she had returned from kennels and I had fretted about how I would manage her. It was then that I saw a photographer from the *Sussex Express*, our local newspaper, taking pictures of some of the dogs. Pleased with our success, I asked if he would like a photo of Connie as she had just won Best Puppy. He obligingly took several shots of her. I also mentioned in passing how she had helped me at home and in the garden since she was small. He looked quite interested to hear about this and made a note of my contact details saying someone from the newspaper might be in touch. Not very likely, I thought, and promptly forgot about it, packing up and heading for home.

Next day Connie and I were happily at home, enjoying the sunshine. I had been gardening and Connie, after rolling in the grass cuttings, was snoozing in the shade. The phone rang and to my surprise it was the *Sussex Express*. They were extremely interested in our story, apparently, and wanted to write a feature on Connie. They said they would be with us in half an hour to interview me and take photos of Connie. I was surprised and, catching sight of myself in the mirror, horrified. There were bits of twig and dead leaves in my hair. The rest of me was a sweaty mess, dressed in baggy old T-shirt and jeans patched with old yellow curtain material. I rather liked those patches which I had cunningly disguised as pockets to hide the holes. Connie was just as bad, her fur a complete contrast to her well-groomed appearance at the show. It was now scruffy and covered in dried grass. There was no way we could face a photographer like this! I flew about dementedly, brushing Connie then manically smartening myself before turning my attention to the cottage. When the journalist and photographer arrived, I was breathless but we were both at least groomed and the house semi-presentable.

Then it struck me: suppose Connie wouldn't perform for the camera? She was used to working quietly for me alone or with just family and friends watching. I felt even more apprehensive when she went wild with excitement, greeting the friendly photographer as an unexpected but very welcome visitor. I needn't have worried, though. After a few manic moments Connie calmed down. With one quiet command from me, she was transformed again into a sensible working dog. It was so instant, it almost seemed like magic. We ran through several of her tasks which she performed faultlessly as if there were no audience.

Just a few days later, there we both were on the front page of the local paper. I was thrilled to see the photo of Connie looking so sweet, pulling off my red Wellington socks. Reading the article, I realised there was one small error in it. Connie only took washing *out* of the machine whereas they had stated that she put it in which is much more difficult to teach. That made me wonder if it was in fact possible, and then of course I had to try. The tumble dryer had a larger door which I thought might make it easier. 'Pick up,' I said, showing Connie a sock in the laundry basket. 'Put in,' I encouraged, at the same time manoeuvring my hand into the drum while holding a piece of chicken. Drop!' I commanded briskly. She obediently dropped the sock into the tumble dryer and I swiftly popped in the treat. Connie quickly caught on and was soon dropping all sorts of items into both the washing machine and tumble dryer. Once she realised what was expected she was happy to be given her reward at the end, after all the clothes were deposited.

At the end of August I was contacted by the *Sussex Argus*, one of the bigger local papers. They'd seen the article in the *Express* and also wanted to run a feature. They took some lovely shots of Connie carrying her basket, on the lawn and on the patio steps, which arrived in time for her first birthday on 1 September. I was thrilled. Connie was such a special dog and gave me such pleasure. Working out how to train her kept me constantly occupied and inspired. I knew it was the sight of her cute funny face and soft brown eyes, imploring me to make the effort, which had urged me on even when it was so difficult for me to just get out of bed.

Connie followed her success at the local dog show with a win at the Newfoundland Club Fun Day which had both breed and obedience classes. Connie and I had worked hard at the various obedience exercises, including the 'stay' command. This was my main concern because there is a great deal of difference between a quiet practice session at home and performing in a ring full of other dogs. It was a lovely drive through the Sussex countryside to the old pub and field where the event was being held, and a great chance to catch up with old friends there and see how their dogs had grown and matured. For her part, Connie was very excited to see so many other dogs like herself. Not much chance for us in obedience, I thought to myself. I'd entered just for the fun and experience. Once again Connie surprised me by just how good she was in her individual exercises. But what about the 'stays'? I was sure she would get up to play with the other dogs. But when the time came, Connie watched me carefully and stayed in position just as if she were at home with me alone. I was quietly pleased, but completely bowled over a little later when it was announced that we had won. It was only a simple obedience test but it involved competing against other Newfoundlands and was one more thing we had achieved together. Cassie had also always done well in the obedience class at the Newfoundland Club, so it felt as if Connie was carrying on a tradition.

At home training continued, with Connie learning to build on old tasks along with taking in some new ones. For instance, at my shout of 'Compost bin', she would take off for the bin hidden away behind our garage, and fetch the waste container back to me. I always had the goodies pot ready with some special treat for her, as without this incentive it would have been too tempting for her to chew the container with all its interesting food smells.

The days were noticeably shortening and the autumn leaves falling fast. It hardly seemed possible that it would soon be Connie's second Christmas with me. We had just one last big project to complete that autumn. Our trusty coal-fired Aga was to be replaced with a new oil-fired one. Even with Connie's help, stoking the coal fire was just too much for me now. Dismantling an Aga is no easy task, and with Fred and Barry set for the day, I decided to take advantage of the fine weather and visit Ashdown Forest for a long walk with Connie. It's not really a forest at all but a vast area of heathland, and one of my favourite places. There are stunning views and interesting tracks. It was there that I had taken Cassie for a poignant last walk when I learned her cancer was untreatable.

Just like all my dogs, Connie finds the forest very exciting and as she's so friendly she especially likes meeting other dogs there. We were walking along one of the tracks with Connie sniffing the air. Gazing ahead, she spotted a pair of Golden Retrievers and galloped on to make friends. I assumed she would soon return as she always did once she had finished playing. I trailed along behind until, rounding a bend in the track, I realised that the Retrievers, their owner and Connie were now a very long way off, almost out of my sight. I called out loudly and, peering ahead, was relieved to see Connie sitting at the side of the track waiting for me. However, when I reached the spot I realised with horror that it was not my beloved dog at all but a shadowy gorse bush. Connie and the other dogs had vanished. I felt sick with worry, running on and calling her name as loudly as I could. There was no sign of her. I was soon desperate. There were tracks branching off and running in all directions. I had no idea which one to follow. I couldn't believe that a responsible dog owner would just walk on with a strange dog without looking back to see if it was accompanied. I checked as many tracks as I could, calling all the while.

I'd soon alerted other dog walkers, asking whether they had seen Connie. At least a Newfoundland is easy to remember and a few people recalled seeing her with other dogs. I knew she was micro-chipped and had a collar with our telephone number on its disc, but she could be anywhere in over 6000 acres of heathland, lost or even worse, stolen. My other fear was of the roads criss-crossing the forest. Frantic and by now in tears, I phoned home. Fred and Barry immediately set out to help me look for her. It occurred to me that perhaps Connie would find her way back to the car and wait for me there so I returned to the car park, hoping against hope.

One person there told me that Connie had joined her dogs for a little while but had then followed another dog and its owner so she had assumed she was theirs. I stayed in the car park, checking with everyone I met, while Fred and Barry searched. Hours had passed and I was numb with fear. I'd begun to believe I wouldn't see her again when suddenly there she was, being led along by a small, pretty blonde lady who also had her own dog with her. By this point, many people knew about the missing Newfoundland and this sweet lady had found her alone in another car park and kindly taken the trouble to bring her safely back to me. Connie was, of course, oblivious to the fuss she'd caused. It was, however, some time before I felt relaxed enough to return to Ashdown Forest.

9

Dog Friends

One spring afternoon passed happily while Sas and I chatted and drank tea, and our two dogs hurled themselves about, romping through the wood and playing in the stream. They chased and rolled one another and generally had a good time. After Sas and Oliver had left, Connie lay down, worn out, dirty and dishevelled, but looking thoroughly happy with herself. I reflected that although Connie generally likes most dogs she meets, she definitely has her favourites and some she likes more than others, Oliver being top of the list. Dogs have preferences, I suppose, just like humans, and not all dogs get on together.

Just a few days before, I'd visited the vet for Connie to have a routine vaccination and had met a dog owner whose poor Lurcher had been badly bitten by another of her dogs. I felt so sorry for it. The Lurcher was in a miserable state with deep bites to his face and ears. I wanted to give some helpful advice – after all my years working as a dog behaviourist, I've come across most types of problem behaviour – but the sad fact is that, even with the best preparation, not all dogs get along.

I first owned two dogs when Fred and I were given Colleen as a wedding present, supposedly to be a mate for Crispin. This never actually worked out but the dogs got on well together from the first. Colleen was also a Golden Retriever, her fur a perfect mid-gold contrast to Crispin's darker shade. The night we brought Colleen home she curled up with Crispin on a blanket and actually sucked the edge like a baby. In fact, she never grew out of the habit. I remember her getting through a number of different blankets. Crispin was then about five years old which is the ideal time for a dog to be introduced to a new puppy. If the older dog is well trained, the puppy will often pick up their good habits automatically. Strangely, however, Colleen hated travelling in the car and in fact hid to avoid it, whereas Crispin loved it so much that at the first indication of a trip out he would pack himself into the car to make sure he wasn't left behind – a habit Colleen never picked up.

She was otherwise a sensitive, biddable, calm dog whose self-appointed role in life was to look after our children, which she did from when they were babies. She would guard the pram and lie between their cots, comforting them when they cried. She was such a gentle dog, always happy to be part of the boys' games, it was obvious that she would be a perfect mother to her own litters. Crispin by contrast was very much my dog. I'd trained and worked with him, and he had been my constant companion since I'd first brought him home. Maybe it was because they were so different that they got on so well. They certainly complemented one another in character.

When Crispin died, Colleen missed him dreadfully, as did I. Acquiring another dog to help fill the void seemed the obvious solution. As I mentioned earlier, I couldn't contemplate taking on another Golden Retriever after Crispin, and so following diligent research Cassie, my first Newfoundland, came into our lives. This worked very well for the family but Colleen was not so happy. At first, and this is quite common with dogs, she thought the puppy had come for the day and was happy to play with her. Then to her horror it dawned on her that the pesky little pup, who constantly wanted to play and do exciting things when Colleen wanted to sleep, was staying. Not altogether surprisingly the older dog would get cross, snap and growl. This was totally out of character for Colleen and I stopped her. It was only later that I realised it's important to let an older dog discipline a puppy as this is a vital part of their socialisation and learning.

My soft-pedalling led to many problems later as Cassie grew to dominate Colleen. When she was mature she definitely wanted to be top dog and could be aggressive to Colleen if we were not careful. I've since learned that having two bitches of a similar size can cause problems. We dealt with the situation by avoiding anything which might trigger aggression from Cassie towards Colleen. Cassie was actually very sweet and never aggressive with any other dog apart from poor Colleen, who was also very mild-tempered, gentle and submissive. The outbreaks of aggression were usually triggered by disputes over possessions, particularly food or toys. To avoid this all toys were removed and the two dogs were fed separately, with no treats or bones. It worked with this pair, but you can never generalise as different things can trigger aggression in other dogs.

After Colleen's death, when David was around the age of seven, I started to feel decidedly broody . . . for a puppy. Eliza was my Friday Advert dog. I noticed a breeder advertising long-haired Miniature Dachshunds and remembered how much I had admired Susie all those years before in Sweden. There seemed no harm in looking, and of course when I arrived at the breeder's home in Tunbridge Wells and saw how immaculate everything was, how beautifully bred the puppies were with an excellent pedigree, it was obvious that I was going to have one. There were only three, two girls and a boy, and just one girl, Eliza, remaining. (Her sister was called Beth.) Although this was her special kennel name and not in keeping with my habit of calling my dogs names beginning with 'C', I liked it so much I decided to keep the name. On that visit I not only saw the puppies and their mother, but their grandmother too. It was a very maternal line of dogs with the grandmother helping to suckle and clean up after the puppies, too. Eliza was absolutely beautiful with silky, golden-red fur. When I collected her at eight weeks old she curled up on my lap, tucking her little black nose under my left arm almost as if hiding her face. She loved doing that, and for the rest of her life would contentedly relax by rolling into a tight ball, with her tail wrapped around and her nose pushed under my arm.

Eliza and Cassie got on well from the start, unlike Colleen and Cassie. I think because Eliza was so small, Cassie never perceived her as a threat and always viewed her almost as a puppy who needed looking after, so there were never any dominance problems between them. Cassie was middle-aged when Eliza appeared which also helped. Because their relationship worked so beautifully – Eliza pined for Cassie after she died – I didn't hesitate to take on another Newfoundland puppy. This was Christie who was always a very big, strong dog and exceptionally lively as a puppy. Eliza was not pleased. She was obviously terrified of this headstrong, bouncy creature.

It took two years before they became good friends. I also decided to make Eliza top dog as it would have been too dangerous to let the Newfoundland be boss. Eliza was fed first, she was allowed in all the best places, and the puppy had to take second place in absolutely everything, including affection. It may seem harsh but this method worked very well and the two dogs got along happily for the rest of their lives together, with the little Dachshund always taking the lead.

It was during the early period when Eliza was unhappy about Christie that I really learned how important it is to give dogs some special 'me' time that is just for them alone. I made a point of playing with each dog individually, using their own toys and favourite games. Eliza was so fond of her playtime that even when she was a very old dog and profoundly deaf she still enjoyed her toy box and games with me, understanding my hand signals instead of words.

Although I never managed to mate her with Crispin, Colleen had two litters with different dogs from the same breeder. In 1974 she was mated to Camrose Octavius and had eight puppies. As Fred was particularly attached to Colleen he chose the names for this litter, calling each puppy after gliders. As we couldn't afford to furnish the dining-room at the time, Colleen had her puppies in there. Fred made a whelping box and set up a heating lamp over it to keep the new arrivals warm. It was very exciting waiting for puppies, especially for the boys who were all very young then. I set up a camp bed in the dining-room when the time came, but the birth was completely straightforward and we didn't need a vet. I'd known from her maternal instincts around the boys that Colleen would be a fantastic mother and she was.

Watching over a litter is a great deal of work, and quite exhausting. You need constantly to make sure the mother is eating enough and that all the puppies are feeding. At three weeks they need extra food, and you have to keep them clean and make various checks, even clipping their nails so that the mother doesn't get scratched. Alongside

Colleen and her puppies I was also looking after my own children, husband, home, Crispin and the chickens I was breeding at the time; so it was very hard work, though worth it. Witnessing Colleen caring for her litter, and the puppies themselves growing and developing, was a wonderful experience and something I wouldn't have missed for the world, in spite of the lack of sleep at times.

As the first litter was so successful I mated Colleen again a couple of years later, this time with a champion Golden Retriever, Camrose Cabus Christopher, who had won thirty-six challenge certificates. The result was seven puppies: Weaver, Farrier, Spinner, Carpenter, Dairymaid, Milkmaid and Shepherdess. The names were my choice this time and I had terrific fun thinking them up. They were registered with the Kennel Club with my own prefix which was Poundsley. I remember it was lovely weather when they arrived and there are some gorgeous photos of the boys in the garden with the puppies, all different shades of creamy yellow and gold. In Golden Retrievers you can tell by the colour of the puppies' ears what their adult colour will be. At the time the very pale creamy colour that is quite common now was not considered an acceptable shade for Kennel Club registration and dogs that colour were not used for breeding. I think the rule was relaxed because Golden Retrievers became so popular as pets, and because they were potentially good show dogs despite the colour.

It is important to socialise puppies well for their future owners, and obviously spending so much time with them means you get very attached to them. All good breeders will be careful about where their puppies go and will vet potential owners thoroughly. After successfully placing Colleen's first litter, we finally had enough money to buy a dining-room carpet and furniture, as well as carpet for the stairs to what we jokingly call the West Wing. The downside was this meant that the second time round there was only the kitchen for Colleen to have her second litter in. We later built the utility room where Connie now sleeps and the spare bedroom-cum-office where I spent so much time thanks to my back problems. With two fully grown dogs, seven puppies and two children (David had yet to make his appearance in the world) there was not too much space for manoeuvring about or normal kitchen activities. Organisation was the key. The boys, though young, were always very responsible with the animals and helped oversee the puppies' feeding in their own boxes when they started on their extra food.

I found it fascinating to watch the litters grow and the characters of the puppies emerge. They were all so different, each puppy a little individual, just like the children in a family. It was also a wonderful chance to study the behaviour of a bitch with her pups, and such a rewarding experience that despite the hard work I was keen to mate Eliza a few years later. I first checked her eyes with a vet as there can be a problem with Miniature Dachshunds, which means any puppies may go blind. Happily all was fine, so we could go ahead and she was mated to Champion Southcliffe Starskey in November 1987. The puppies were born in January the next year but the birth was not as straightforward as it had been for Colleen.

By then we had built the utility room and I placed the special whelping box for Eliza in there. It was quite a public room and something of a thoroughfare, with Cassie wandering about. Eliza showed signs of wanting to give birth under the bed in the office but I didn't think that was very suitable and discouraged her. With hindsight I made a big mistake and really think I should have let her follow her instincts as once she was in the whelping box her labour just seemed to stop. In the end we had to rush her to the vet where two beautiful puppies, a boy and girl, were delivered by caesarean section. We named these two Bruis and Betsy and for years I had lovely regular updates on Betsy from her owner, Mrs Bevan, who would telephone and pretend to be Betsy Bevan telling me all about her life. As committed dog lovers, we enjoyed the charade!

Having just two puppies in the litter meant they really became part of the family and it was very difficult parting with them both. There was something unbelievably cute about those two small dogs obediently sitting and staying at my command. Mrs Bevan was obviously an ideal owner but, as I've said, I realised early on just how important it is to vet every potential owner and to supervise visitors to the puppies. We had one near-disaster when a visiting child dropped one of Colleen's puppies on to the paving stones. Luckily there was no harm done but I'd learned my lesson and was much more vigilant afterwards.

Two years later we again mated Eliza, this time to a smaller stud dog from the same breeder, called Southcliffe Sovereign. I foolishly repeated my previous mistake, never thinking about where the whelping box should be placed, and again labour started then stopped. Again we rushed Eliza to the vet for another emergency caesarean and this time there were four puppies, one boy and three girls. We named them Prospect, Prunella, Priddie and Pristine, to go with my Kennel Club prefix Poundsley. Sadly this was to be Eliza's last litter and to this day I regret not keeping one of her puppies. There is nothing more comforting than a small Dachshund, curled around and snuggled up, keeping you company on the sofa.

Eliza loved holidays away with us, digging in the sand and playing on the beach while keeping well away from any water, which she hated. Having spent so much time with larger dogs, I believe she thought of herself as a big Newfoundland rather than a small Dachshund. Certainly on the beach one day when a Great Dane dared to approach her, she saw him off in no time. It was very funny to watch this tiny dog chasing the baffled gentle giant away. However, unlike my Newfoundlands, Eliza did not like strangers stroking her and was always very shy with people until she really got to know them.

If all my years of experience have taught me anything it is that all dogs are different, with their own idiosyncrasies, likes and dislikes, no matter what breed or sex. Even dogs from the same litter can be completely opposite characters. Some get along, and some do not. But with a little thought and planning I've found it is possible to avoid major problems and encourage even reluctant twosomes to find a way to live together happily.

10

Troubleshooting

Having always enjoyed training my own dogs, I first began working to help other people with theirs over twenty years ago. David had just started playschool and I wanted something to do which would earn me a little money and allow me the freedom to work from home at times which suited my family life. I also needed to earn some extra money to keep the chickens I bred through the winter before I could sell the young stock and chicks in the spring.

I placed an advertisement in a local newspaper, offering individual dog-training lessons. I really didn't have any great expectations and so was very surprised when my phone hardly stopped ringing with enquiries over the next few weeks. It seemed that many people did not enjoy group lessons and much preferred the more personal one-to-one sessions I could offer. And so my career as a dog trainer began. Later, I increasingly concentrated on sorting out behavioural problems as I found this gave me more flexibility and I enjoyed the challenge. I was working as a behaviourist before the term was really coined for use in connection with dogs, and it's satisfying to see that the same positive reinforcement methods I was using all those years ago are now regarded as the norm.

From the start, I tried to keep the training sessions fun

and simple. I always varied the content – for instance, there would be no continuous repetition of heel work until it was perfect. Instead I taught several things at the same time, mixing heel work with finding, retrieving and holding. I tried a variety of exercises, keeping them short to maintain the dogs' interest. I've always found that using rewards works better than imposing your will on a dog – hence the special goodies pot when I'm teaching Connie anything new or difficult today. With puppies I often began with an old sock which I would wave around to make it appear exciting, and when the dog couldn't wait to grab it, I would introduce the word 'Hold' so they would begin to associate the word with the action. I'm always lavish with praise, so there would be lots of 'Good dog' when a dog had successfully held the sock. Then I would rustle a bag of treats or bounce a ball to divert the dog's attention so they would go for that and drop the sock conveniently into my hand, at which point I would say 'Give'. At the end, I made sure there was time for the dog to play and would talk to the owner about their dog's progress.

One young Pointer who came to me in the early days so enjoyed his lessons that his owners had to spell out my name. If they forgot and said 'Hazel' aloud, he would race around the house like a maniac. While the lessons were taking place, I kept my own dogs out of the way, but at the end, during the play session they would usually all romp around together which was a useful addition to the young dogs' socialisation.

Although I really enjoyed taking on new owners and young puppies and gradually guiding them through training, I found these lessons were taking up a great deal of my time. I never seemed to lose any clients. Instead they kept on coming, for a year or more. In many ways this was lovely and I made some very good friends whom I still see, but I decided to concentrate on behavioural work which would mean just a few sessions, either at my cottage or the owner's home. This meant I was often dealing with problem dogs. I would always talk to the owners at some length before meeting the dog, to ascertain exactly what the problem was and whether the dog was likely to be aggressive. If there seemed a likelihood of that, I would always suggest they came to me at the cottage where I could retreat into my utility room. The ever-useful baby gates offered me vital protection.

Things didn't get off to the best start. The first call I had was about a large guard dog of six months. The owners described him as very powerful and mentioned that he sometimes bit. Mr and Mrs Jones duly arrived with Rex. I bravely took his lead and at first was pleasantly impressed. He walked well to heel, and when I said 'Sit' he obediently did so. I began to relax, thinking he really wasn't a problem, when without warning he growled and showed his teeth. He really was a huge, strong dog and I am not very big. Nevertheless we made a few more circuits but he was completely unpredictable and in truth I was terrified. I felt that I was out of my depth with him, as there seemed to be some underlying psychological problem in his case. Reluctantly, as I never like to give up on an animal, I recommended that Rex should be checked by a vet – not an auspicious beginning.

The next visit didn't go much better. A minister and his mother had each bought a black and white Collie cross from the same litter and were having problems with them being aggressive. I began by trying to teach them to retrieve a ball. They didn't quite manage it and, as I bent down to pick up the ball, one of the dogs lunged forward to bite my head. He got away with an alarmingly big mouthful of my hair. On their next visit, Fred came home from working at the airport still in his uniform to which the dogs took an instant dislike. My husband beat a timely retreat. Next time I was properly kitted out. Wearing long leather gauntlets, I eventually began to get somewhere with the dogs who basically needed to be kept busy and working. I suggested various tasks, similar to some of the more simple things that Connie does for me now, to keep the pair of them interested and out of mischief.

There was also a lively young Labrador who was so beside himself with excitement when we began heel work that he kept pulling at and ripping his owner's expensive-looking sheepskin coat. I was definitely more concerned than his owner, who appeared oblivious to the damage.

I followed this with a very lively but good-natured Great Dane called Darcy. After a successful beginning, we were working on practical exercises in the field, using an expanding lead. I let it out as far as it would go, with Darcy happily running round and round, until I realised I needed rescuing as I was wound up like a cocoon!

Another time I was asked to see one of the boys' teachers who had a dog called Lucy who would not come when called. As soon as the car door opened, Lucy shot out and headed for the wood where she remained for the whole of the first session.

One method I use to encourage dogs to return willingly to their owners when called, or for a dog which is reluctant or perhaps fearful of getting into a car, is to ask the owner to park their car in the garden outside my house where it is safe. The owner and dog then come inside the house. Later I ask the owner to return to their car, leaving one of the doors open. The dog is left behind with me. After a few minutes I tell the owner to call their dog and I let it outside. Invariably the dog is so pleased to be reunited with their owner that they rush straight outside and happily jump into the car.

I tried another method with Lucy which was for me to hold on to her lead while her owner walked away across the field, rustling a bag of treats and remaining in the dog's line of vision. By the time her owner called her excitedly and I released Lucy from her lead she was desperate to rush off to her owner. I used this same method with another dog that had not been let off his lead in two years because his owner was so concerned he would fail to come when called and then she would lose him. I have found this method generally works very effectively in fixing the idea of coming when called, and I have successfully used several variations on it.

I found that I often had to work around the owners' fixed ideas first. They would often begin by saying that their dog would never sit, or play, or eat treats, whereas I usually found they just needed a little encouragement or a slightly different approach. I've always found that offering treats really speeds up training. As I've said, I use a rustling bag with treats inside so that I can make a noise with it and let the dog sniff it. At first I will rustle the bag but won't let the dog have what's inside until he is really interested. I will then offer him a treat when he sits.

I really enjoy home visits as they are such a good opportunity to see a dog in its own environment and assess their true character. One elderly couple I visited owned a Jack Russell Yorkie cross bitch called Scruff who was very lively and barked constantly. I've found over the years that it's often the smaller dogs, and particularly terriers, that cause the worst problems with noise. I always ask lots of questions and just observe for a long time before making any suggestions. As the owners and I drank tea and chatted, Scruff jumped around, barking incessantly. I suggested we should all make a big fuss of her whenever she was briefly quiet and ignore her completely when she made a noise. After causing mayhem for two years with this behaviour, for the last half an hour of my visit Scruff was quiet. I also successfully use this simple technique of ignoring bad behaviour and praising good to stop dogs making a fuss or even biting their owners to gain their attention. Distracting them with a toy or chew also helps.

Whenever there is a bad incident involving a dog there are always cries from the public and the media that it is the dog owner's fault. Sometimes this is the case, but this is not necessarily so. There are many reasons why dogs behave badly, or demonstrate what we now tend to call 'unwanted behaviour'. A lot of people are bombarded with often conflicting and very bad advice on training and 'punishment'. This can be very confusing, especially for the new and inexperienced owner. It is bad enough people suggesting very harsh outdated methods, but it is much worse when it is the trainers at puppy parties or instructors at dog-training classes who actually cause a serious behavioural problem. Sometimes they insist on removing the dog from its bewildered owner, to demonstrate a new training method or show how to punish it. For example, one young dog was taken to a new training club when his owner moved house. He had been happy and relaxed with both the members and instructors at his last club but was very worried when confronted with strange dogs and a different hall. The new instructor took the nervous dog away from his owner and tried to force him into the 'down' position which the dog resisted. Panicking, the frightened animal then growled, whereupon he was hit and pushed violently to the floor, hitting his head. This experience for a young dog was so traumatic that he became aggressive with strangers and, after biting someone who put their hand out to stroke him, was very sadly put to sleep.

Sometimes it is circumstances beyond the control of the owner that trigger unwanted behaviour, such as illness or depression. One lady I helped had put her little terrier into kennels for two weeks while she was on holiday. The dog, who was young and lively, had a kennel with run attached to live in. Normally a couple of weeks kept in these conditions would be fine but the owner did not return to collect her dog for six months because she was taken seriously ill on holiday. Needless to say, this little dog was really wild and out of control when it returned home.

Another lady had recently bought a Spaniel puppy before she sadly had a stroke which left her with speech and mobility problems. I always remember her being very upset and saying she had failed her dog because she had not trained it as well as she would have liked.

Moving house, changing jobs or partners, or the addition of new human or canine members to the family, can seriously upset some dogs. They then show they are stressed by barking when left, causing problems with neighbours, pooing on beds, wetting on carpets and chewing up furniture, especially the item on which their favourite person sits, as the comforting scent helps relieve their stress.

Dogs from the same litter can have a wide range of temperaments. I know a family where the son had one Labrador puppy while his mother had another from the same litter. They lived close by and both dogs had the same upbringing. The mother's dog was quiet and placid; the son's dog's aim in life was to attack other dogs!

Another interesting case was where two people in the same road had puppies from the same litter. Both were well socialised but one was very timid and nervous with people. The other puppy from the litter had a similar background but was bold and outgoing. It can be a shock for someone if they have always had biddable, easily trained Labradors to discover that their new puppy is more like a devilish fiend than an angelic Andrex puppy. When people have children, however, they readily accept that their offspring may have totally different characters even though they are reared in the same environment with the same house rules. Dogs can have similar natural variations in temperament, which can lead to behavioural problems if not taken into account.

Sometimes problems seem to arise suddenly with previously well-behaved dogs. One busy family I visited had a young Cocker Spaniel who had suddenly started chewing the kitchen units at night. I discovered this had begun when an elderly aunt came to stay in the bedroom near the kitchen where Bella, the Spaniel, slept. The aunt got up frequently in the night and the sudden change in routine had stressed Bella. Although the aunt left, the chewing continued; in fact, she completely destroyed their old kitchen. The family had now had a smart new one fitted and were very concerned to make sure that Bella did not start chewing this one. I have sometimes found that dogs can be more relaxed if they sleep closer to the rest of the family and suggested leaving Bella in the sitting-room at night when they went to bed.

Calling back a few days later, I asked, 'How's Bella getting along?' confident of a positive response. The husband answered, 'It's terrible, she's ruined our new kitchen.' He sounded so upset and cross, I was devastated. 'I am sorry,' I muttered apologetically. There was then the sound of muffled laughter from the other end of the room, which was a little strange, I thought. 'I was joking! We followed your suggestions and everything is fine now,' Bella's owner chuckled gleefully.

One Christmas a worried owner telephoned me sounding extremely upset because her two Border Collies seemed intent on killing each other. They had always been the best of friends before this so it was a great shock for her to return from a pre-Christmas holiday to find the pair fighting. I soon realised the reason for the dogs' sudden aggression. While the owner was away, her mother had moved into the family's home to look after the dogs. The problem was simply that she had fed the lower-ranking dog first, which had enraged the top dog. When the family came back, the former underdog was desperate to hold on to his new position and was ready to fight for it. As a temporary emergency measure muzzling can help, but the important thing is a speedy return to the routine that had previously worked. In this case, once the pecking order was carefully restored, the dogs were friends again.

During my work as a behaviourist, I have come across a number of what I refer to as Jekyll and Hyde dogs. They appear absolutely lovely, calm and well trained – except for the instant when they suddenly change character. Sadly, I have seen this type of split personality in several Golden Retrievers. I think this is largely because they are so popular that there is now a great deal of breeding, often using stud dogs with none of the once-common hip problems but with far from certain temperaments.

So it is essential to choose your breeder carefully. Make sure they're reputable and Kennel Club-registered, and check both parent dogs. One lovely female Golden Retriever called Meg seemed wonderful until the moment when she was put to bed when she would growl ferociously. My solution was to ignore her when she was in her bed and for a time avoid going near it. Another dog hated it when their owner was on the phone and continually tugged on the arm of their sweater or growled if they dared to move away. I suggested keeping a favoured squeaky toy or chew ready so that next time the phone rang the dog could be rewarded with the toy before he reacted. Dogs barking when their owners are talking on the phone is a common problem, probably because people tend to rush to answer it and dogs copy their owner and get excited. I would suggest tackling this problem in the same way. In both cases, it is important to remain calm and take no notice of the bad behaviour.

The next most frequent cause of problems are the destroyers. They are often Labradors and one of the first I saw was a very big strong dog called Max. It was a wild, windy day outside when he arrived, crashing in through the hallway, barging into the table and scattering my notes everywhere. He then turned his attention to me, launching himself at me and almost knocking me over in his ebullience. He was not nasty-tempered, just good at demolition, and when he nearly cracked the glass on one of my pictures I'd really had enough. I suggested we put him back in the car for a short time while we finished talking over his problems in peace. The exhausted owner looked dubious but Max was duly shut back in her car while we kept an eye on him from the kitchen window. He looked peaceful enough but soon it was hard to see clearly through the rain-lashed windows. He was there for less than five minutes but when we collected him, Max had thoroughly chewed his lead and, worse, shredded the driver's seat. His owner looked rather shocked and I couldn't believe he'd done so much damage in such a short time. Needless to say, I have never made that suggestion again.

I visited Alfie, another Labrador, when he was sixteen months old. He was an extremely handsome black dog but very naughty. Alfie destroyed on a grand scale and had removed all the plaster within his reach from a rather elegant plaster archway in his home. The walls, skirting boards, window and door frames all bore the marks of his attention. Then he had moved on to the garden where he had chewed the exterior window sills, a garden wall and a rabbit hutch (luckily without a rabbit inside). Watching him, I realised he was an intelligent dog but probably bored by inactivity. He needed to be working so I suggested play and training to keep him fully occupied and teach him a skill like agility work. He proved to be very good at this and loved it. Over time his behaviour was transformed.

Two dogs in the same household can also spell trouble, as I had discovered with my own twosomes. One owner had two young yellow Labradors who were so alike they had to wear different-coloured collars to distinguish them. Unfortunately, Alice, their owner, had been advised not to train the dogs until they were six months old, which is always a mistake. This pair had chewed through kitchen units and doors. They helped themselves to their own dog food, ripping open the bags and spilling the contents on the floor. They stole their owner's food too and even filched from pans still on the cooker. Outside they had ruined the French doors, dug holes in the lawn, and almost killed a lovely old birch tree by stripping off the bark. As well as this trail of devastation, they were not toilet-trained and simply freely used the area behind the kitchen door, which defied description.

Alice knew the problem was out of hand. She had thought that two young dogs the same age would keep each other amused and out of trouble. In actual fact having two puppies together can create problems. There is the danger of them acquiring a pack mentality when they will exacerbate each other's bad behaviour. Training also needs to begin from day one. With my own litters, even when the puppies were very young, I always gently corrected and trained – using my standard rule of praising positive behaviour and ignoring bad, just the way I would treat the terrible twos in toddlers. Faced with these two six-month-old delinquents, training had to start from scratch, including toilet training as a priority. Of course, by this stage it's not so easy because the dogs have developed bad habits which have to be unlearned and corrected while they are effectively wilful adolescents.

Part of the reason why I've seen so many Labradors is

because they are such a popular breed, and for good reason. They generally make excellent family pets: they are friendly, loyal, biddable and intelligent, and not difficult to train well. It's not surprising they are often chosen to be guide dogs as they can be very sensitive to their owners' needs and moods, but they are often of working stock and do need to be kept busy. It's worth remembering that they are highly motivated by food and fuss. They like to play and adore being with their owners – they love people and get very lonely when left for any length of time.

Dogs and their owners can still sometimes surprise me. Not so long ago a rather prim lady brought her German Shepherd, Daisy, to me. We sat at the kitchen table, discussing her training and behavioural problems. Daisy seemed to me extremely well behaved. After a very brief investigation of the kitchen, she settled down quietly next to us. Before long, though, I began to notice a particularly nasty smell which, if anything, was growing stronger. I gave my visitor a side-long glance and realised she was doing the same to me. Neither of us mentioned the by now very pungent odour. When it was time to take Daisy outside for some practice lead work, I cleared away our coffee cups and walked to the other side of the island unit where I immediately found the source of the stench – a huge pile of foul-smelling dog poo. I still don't know how Daisy had managed to slip quietly round there without our noticing.

Occasionally it seems to be the owners who have the problems rather than their dogs. One lady I visited whose Airedale seemed fine to me obviously wanted someone to talk to. From the first she appeared agitated and unsettled. After several phone calls to her husband, his office and secretary, and finally a hotel (all made from the next room but impossible not to overhear), it became apparent that he was having an affair. I assume she didn't want to be alone when she found out for certain. She had no wish to discuss her own problems and focussed on her dog while she was with me. I think she just wanted a sympathetic ear. I made my excuses and left when her husband rang back and she began a very heated argument with the errant spouse.

Another home visit was to a working farm one wet winter's day. On arrival I was greeted by half a dozen very muddy Jack Russell puppies, all keen to jump up at me. Inside the farm kitchen there seemed to be little Jack Russells sitting on every available armchair, most busily tugging and pulling all the stuffing from the cushions. The air was thick with it, feathers and foam floating about almost like snow. Ah ha! I thought. I didn't need to be a detective to realise what the problem was here. However, I was wrong. When the chairs became too badly damaged to use, the farmer and his wife simply bought more of them. Their objection was to the way some of the dogs fought one another, and they wanted my help in calming the feuding.

Before setting out on a behaviour consultation visit I ponder the problems ahead. Will I have to deal with nervousness, perhaps bad temper, frustration, extreme anxiety, or another very worrying issue – the dreaded toileting problems? These are just some of the behavioural problems I myself face as I drive to visit my canine clients: finding my way through strange places, busy roads, trying to find the right address and arrive on time!

It was after a particularly difficult journey where I had been looking for a loo that I eventually arrived to see Ben, a young and excitable yellow Labrador. Rather embarrassed, I hurriedly asked if I could use the loo and shot up the stairs with the dog galloping behind me. He thought it would be fun to keep me company in the bathroom but I quickly shut the door before he could push his way in. I could relax at last, until I looked round for the toilet paper: first a casual glance, then a good look, then a frantic search everywhere but there was definitely no loo paper in the bathroom. Eventually I returned to the owners who were patiently waiting for me. 'I'm afraid I couldn't find any toilet paper', I whispered. 'That's why we wanted you to come. Ben is always stealing the loo rolls and is very clever at finding them in even our most inventive hiding places!'

Another visit was to see a young Labrador cross bitch called Betty who was rather wild and out of control, and in her spare time liked to continue her self-appointed task of demolishing her owners' little garden.

I went into the kitchen and met the owner's middle-aged daughter who had asked me to call. The dog seemed delighted to see a visitor and charged at me with an enthusiastic welcome, nearly knocking me over. I was then introduced to the daughter's rather elderly mother who said hello in a very quavery voice. She was trying to make herself some toast and a cup of tea but Betty thought it would be fun to try to knock the tea over and snatch the toast. 'Betty, get down! Stop it and go to bed,' the lady said hopefully, but Betty took no notice. In the end, hanging on precariously to her tea and toast, the poor lady retreated into the sitting-room which was next to the kitchen. Betty stayed in the kitchen with us.

I attempted to proceed with my consultation with the daughter, but this did not last long. Betty, with a wicked gleam in her eye, launched herself at the table, scattering my notes, upsetting my tea and jumping all over me. It was chaotic. At this point the daughter grabbed Betty by the collar and put her in the sitting-room with her long-suffering mother. I rather hoped she had finished her tea and toast by then. After a minute or so there was a thunderous pounding on the door leading back to the kitchen. I heard the now-familiar quavering voice say, 'Betty, get down! Stop it and go to bed.' There was perhaps a second of

114

silence before the next onslaught on the door which sounded as though a battering ram was being used. Again Betty was told to get down, stop it and go to bed; needless to say she took no notice at all.

At this point I decided I would have to say something about the elderly lady's training methods. I tactfully and politely suggested to the daughter that the dog would not learn if her mother kept repeating commands but did not insist on the dog carrying out the orders. 'Oh, that's not my mother talking to Betty in there,' said the daughter, sounding rather surprised. 'That's the parrot.'

Time and again I see the same problems arising between dogs and their owners: pulling on the lead; a reluctance to come when called or perhaps to travel in the car; trouble with 'play' biting which is very rarely aggressive and much more a case of seeking attention. I see my role very much as that of a mediator or counsellor, sorting out the relationship between dog and human, encouraging people to be more confident in the way they respond. My basic strategy is always the same no matter what the problem. I look for the reasons behind the behaviour. Dogs do not learn if they are afraid, stressed or in pain, nor if they are either too excited or bored. Keeping them interested and rewarded helps learning, and it's useful to remember that most dogs are motivated by one or more of the four Fs – food, fuss, freedom and fun to a greater or lesser degree.

I try to desensitise whatever problem has arisen by very gradual exposure to the root cause of the trouble, with positive reinforcements along the way to build confidence. Distraction with a toy, food or attention diverts the dog from whatever it is he is thinking of doing – this is particularly helpful with barking or biting. Once a dog has learned certain unwanted behaviour, if it is not reinforced by the owner's reaction or reward it will gradually be eliminated.

If necessary, one can try 'time out'. This simply means leaving the room for a few minutes when the dog misbehaves, returning and then carrying on as normal. If the time out method fails, simply ignoring the dog and avoiding eye contact also works well.

I've often heard owners commenting that when their dog has chewed their possessions or messed in the house he is teaching them a lesson, or taking revenge. This is rarely the case. Dogs really are not 'being bad' nor are they 'expressing guilt'. The dog is simply reacting to our body language, disapproving actions and attitude, and it is this which leads him to look guilty. He does not know he has been bad and is understandably worried and fearful when confronted by an angry owner.

Ripping clothes and wetting on them is a very typical response of a dog who has been left alone and is suffering from stress and anxiety. After doing this, he may well have curled up and gone to sleep. When the owner returns later and is understandably upset to find the mess, the dog is confused, thinking he is being punished for sleeping which in turn causes more stress and anxiety, exacerbating the problem. You can find my problem solving strategies for specific behaviour on page 167.

Having helped so many dogs with behavioural problems, which have often arisen as a result of stress or upheaval, it is no wonder I was so concerned about the effect my illness and her time away might have on Connie. As I write this, she is as usual lying curled up beside me, relaxed and contented. She has that doggy smell she gets after a long ramble through the wood and a swim in a rather murky farm pond, and will need a bath and thorough grooming to untangle her coat later on. 'You smell just like sweaty damp football boots, Connie,' I tell her. She gazes up at me adoringly, wagging her tail in agreement, completely happy with her lot.

11

Whatever the Weather

On 1 January 2007 I woke with a feeling of keen anticipation. A new year lay ahead and, as usual, I had
plans – many revolving around Connie, her training, and
how we might progress even further. It would have been
odd if I hadn't thought back to the start of the previous
year, too, and how all my optimistic plans then had been
swept aside. But we had come through that and, if anything,
were stronger as a result. Life was good, I thought, sitting
up in bed enjoying my early morning cup of tea.

The flocks of long-tailed tits which had given me such
a lovely surprise, arriving in time for my birthday in
December, were still very much in evidence, clustering about
our bird feeders. Pheasants strutted the fields and lanes,
noisily clucking a protest whenever they were disturbed.
Early in the year is the best time to work in our wood
clearing away brambles, well before the bluebells emerge
or there's any danger of disturbing the ground nesting birds.
I learned to scythe efficiently while I was at Brinsbury
Training Farm, and still really enjoy wielding a mattock.
There's something so satisfying and calming about the
swishing motion of scything, quite unlike using a noisy
electric trimmer which cuts so indiscriminately. I can take
my time with the hand scythe and watch what I'm doing.

It's lucky I do for as I cut away a dense clump of under-growth, I uncovered a large, coiled snake. I'd inadvertently disturbed his winter's sleep and, angry at the disturbance, he reared up, hissing. I carefully covered him again with a thick layer of dead bracken and retreated.

As the winter light faded away in mid-afternoon, it was satisfying to see the results of my hard labour. At a word from me, Connie, always my willing assistant, rushed up to take the bucket containing my gloves and tools. We walked back companionably to the cottage with the winter sun setting low in the sky. The kitchen lights were glowing invitingly and I knew the Aga would be warm and comforting, ready for me to pop in the scones I'd made earlier for tea. My pace quickened at the prospect.

Once inside, Connie helped me take off my coat and socks, then fetched my indoor shoes. 'Towel, Connie,' prompted her to jump up and retrieve her towel from the top of the washing machine. 'Sit,' and she obediently did, offering me each paw in turn to dry. 'Stand, good girl,' I said, noticing that her towel now needed washing. 'Wash box,' I said and Connie gathered up the towel and dropped it carefully into the laundry basket. After all this, I gave her her well-deserved treat and made tea and scones for myself.

Just as I had hoped, that January also brought snow. Connie was now big enough to pull a light sledge and so the old wooden one the boys had loved to play with had been fitted with new metal runners to make it glide smoothly over the snow. I also had a harness ready, beautifully made especially for her by a friend of mine. Connie now had her thick oily adult coat with its double layer of fur: a dense undercoat and longer topcoat, to insulate and waterproof. It is this thick undercoat which sheds, particularly in spring, and makes grooming Newfoundlands such hard work.

Connie looked very smart in her harness when I tried it on her. I was not sure what she would make of it but she seemed quite content to let me adjust it so it fitted her perfectly. Now to introduce the sledge.

To begin with, I pulled it while Connie walked beside me. The next step was to clip her to it and set off again. At first I pulled a little as well so that Connie could gradually get used to it before taking all the weight. Then, with the extra incentive of some especially tasty treats and an encouraging 'Pull!' we were really off. Connie quickly learned the 'Pull' and 'Stop' commands and walked around our two little fields.

It was a perfect winter's day with a clear blue sky and the sun shining down on crisp unmarked snow. I didn't want to tire Connie on her first attempt with the sledge. So, after a short session, I unharnessed her so that she could enjoy frolicking in the snow. She galloped around madly then rolled over and over until she was smothered in powdery snow. She gave herself a quick shake before she was off again, leaping and bounding in boisterous appreciation. I threw one of her squeaky toys into a snowdrift whereupon Connie plunged her fluffy black head eagerly under the snow to find it. Strange to think that she really doesn't feel the cold beneath that wonderful fur coat. In fact, it's heat that is the problem. I'm very careful to make sure she doesn't get too hot and has plenty of water to drink.

I've always loved the snow and Newfoundlands are the perfect dogs to share it with. Maybe it's the golden glow of nostalgia but I'm sure there used to be more snow when our sons were growing up and it definitely lasted longer. As David was the youngest and lightest, my first Newfoundland, Cassie, would pull him up the hill on his sledge, then he and his brothers would whizz down again, shrieking with laughter, Cassie joining in the general mayhem. One amazing winter it snowed so much that our valley was completely cut off, all four lanes blocked by snowdrifts, and no cars able to get in or out. A willing Cassie pulled David on his sledge along the snowy lanes in total safety. One year, the snow was so deep the wind had whipped it into drifts that banked up level with the tops of the hedges. Eliza's short little legs hardly dinted the surface as she half trotted, half skipped along the top where the hedgerow should have been. Eliza always enjoyed the snow although she hated the rain and wet.

Connie and I were able to have one more outing with the sledge before the snow completely melted away. She seemed to know instinctively what to do and I wondered if it was because of some genetic memory from her ancestors way back in Canada. As well as helping fishermen with their nets and rescuing sailors, Newfoundlands were also used to haul lumber and pull carts. At one time they were a common sight, delivering the mail as well as milk, and they also carried other loads in packs. They were so successful in Poole in Dorset that horse-and-cart owners were concerned they would be put out of business and complained that the dogs barked too much. It is said that the carters had greater political clout and so Newfoundlands were banned from haulage – whether this is true or not it's hard to tell, but I like the story.

Our Newfoundlands have lived up to their reputation and always helped out over the years with heavy work. At the time of the great hurricane which swept across South East England in October 1987, Cassie was a strong, mature eight year old. I remember lying awake that night listening to the wind roaring while Cassie, Eliza and David slept through oblivious to any danger. At the time we didn't realise just how terrible it was as the roar of the storm drowned out the sound of the trees crashing down all around, but I was horribly aware of the danger from the huge oaks and

120

silver birches which grew so close to the cottage and, I realised with a sudden jolt, towered over David's room.

I raced upstairs, shouting, 'Wake, wake up!' pulling at my son's arm and shaking him urgently. He stirred and mumbled sleepily, completely unaware that anything was wrong. He carried on grumbling as I dragged him to his feet and propelled him downstairs to the relative safety of the kitchen where we all sat round the table waiting apprehensively for the dawn.

Looking outside next morning I was shocked to see daylight where there used to be trees. The devastation was incredible. A huge swathe of our wood was gone, as if a giant scythe had sliced through it in the night. Trees had been torn up by the roots and huge branches littered the drive and garden. When I stepped outside I realised with a shock how lucky we had been. A great bough had crashed through the garage roof but none of the trees which grow close to the house had fallen, including the two birches which could have crushed David's room. At the time I kept chickens and the 28' x 9' roof of the large hen house in the field had been ripped off and tossed into the next field. Fortunately, there were no birds inside, as all the chickens were in the small portable chicken houses. These had also been flung about but not really damaged. Amazingly only two hens had been killed. The survivors were clucking indignantly and making a huge fuss, but soon quietened down once their houses had been righted and I'd settled them with plenty of fresh straw, food and water.

In the lane, fallen electrical cables had become tangled in the torn branches and toppled trees, and it was hard to find a way through safely. With all the usual landmarks gone it was easy to become completely disorientated but Eliza, with her great nose for tracking, always knew exactly where she was and we learned to rely on her to lead us.

We had lost so many trees from our wood that it was unrecognisable. It was heartbreaking to see ancient oak, beech and silver birch simply ripped from the ground, their huge rootballs exposed and deep craters yawning where they had once grown – so fixed and, I'd thought, immovable. When we began the clear-up in the aftermath of the storm, the sound of our chainsaw was echoed across the valley from all sides as others began the same sad task.

Cassie helped so much pulling the heavier branches and logs or carrying them in her mouth. When we finally got out past our lane the gashes in the countryside were starkly obvious and the smell of wood smoke permeated the air. As the first winter now fell, Cassie pulled sledgeloads of logs to the house for us.

It seemed impossible at first that the woodland could ever recover, yet the area has regenerated remarkably, so that now the only reminder of the devastation are the few remaining rootballs where foxes have made their dens and rabbits have burrowed. Just recently Connie dug down and uncovered a huge rabbit hole where a tree had obviously once stood until the hurricane. One casualty in our wood was the bluebells which disappeared for several years, though I'm happy to say they have since returned and in even greater numbers, so that once again in early-spring the woods are carpeted with blue and scented with their wonderful forest perfume.

We were luckier than many people at the time because we still had our trusty Aga for warmth and somewhere to cook. With all the cables torn down there was no electricity for three weeks and no phone for six. A part of me revelled in those lamplit evenings, spent playing card games or chess since there was no TV. The candles and the smell of the oil lamps reminded me of childhood evenings in the cottage at West Harting, with family and dogs all enjoying the warmth of the kitchen. We recreate something of the same atmosphere on winter evenings now, with the curtains drawn and a log fire burning. Connie nestles against me for her evening ritual of cuddles and fuss. As I stroke her soft chest she appears to be in an almost trance-like state, leaning against me with eyes half closed in utter bliss, her velvet face and ears resting on my lap.

A few days after the snow melted, my friend Sas and Connie's play-mate Oliver came to visit. A tall pine tree had recently crashed down and Fred had sawn it up into manageable logs ready to store. They were still piled up outside along with mounds of fresh, pungent sawdust and shavings. Sas and I watched our two dogs tear through the wood and splash into the stream then bound back to the pile of logs. I remembered Cassie sensibly pulling her sledgeloads of logs after the hurricane, and then watched Connie madly rolling in the shavings, romping with Oliver, tumbling over and over until she had sawdust plastered into her long fur, in her ears, around her eyes and all over her face. Oliver's sleek black fur was still relatively neat by comparison.

The next day I noticed a small swelling on her face, and then a second. More appeared almost as I watched. By the following morning her face was covered in large suppurating blisters. They were so bad that her eyes had almost disappeared. I was horrified and immediately telephoned the vet. Once at the surgery, Connie was her usual bouncy self. I'm afraid she generally misbehaves there. Unlike many dogs, she loves going to see the vet. One word of welcome from the receptionist is enough to encourage her up on to the desk for a friendly greeting. This time she quickly spotted a small dog and took a dive towards him to make friends. I tried to pull her back in case her condition was catching. The vet thoroughly examined Connie but was puzzled about the cause of the blisters. It is possible they were a reaction to the sap oozing from the logs and wood shavings, though luckily Oliver was fine. They eventually cleared up after a course of antibiotics and, although they looked nasty, Connie seemed completely untroubled by them.

She was much more upset by a frightening incident which happened at home not long afterwards. Connie had always drunk from a bowl placed beneath the outside water tap and, thirsty after a walk, went for her usual drink. She suddenly yelped, screamed loudly and ran away. She was obviously in pain and very frightened. To my dismay, I found the tap, water and metal drinking bowl were all live due to an electrical fault. Fred is an aeronautical engineer and quickly found and fixed the problem but Connie has never forgotten her shock. She used to like lying in this shady spot but has never done so since the accident. It took several months before she would reluctantly drink from the same bowl and then only if it was placed well away from its original position beneath the tap.

The after-effects of fear or pain can be extremely long-lasting and in some cases the dog never forgets, especially if they were very young when the trauma occurred. The memory of my first experience of a dog being badly frightened still upsets me. It happened to Crispin when he was just five months old. He was lying waiting for me while I collected a bucket of virtually boiling water. It was dark and I did not see him. I tripped and fell so that poor Crispin was hit by me, the bucket and the very hot water. Luckily he was not badly hurt but he was extremely shaken. Years later I worked him in top obedience competitions and demonstrations. He was very capable and would carry practically anything I asked – except for a bucket.

12

A Setback

At the beginning of February, just over a year after my back problems first began, I had my final appointment with the specialist who declared me fully fit. He explained that I was bound to get some pain after exercise but that was nothing to worry about. 'Can I do lots of gardening?' I immediately asked. 'That's fine, you can do what you want,' the consultant replied, adding with a smile, 'I don't want to see you again.'

I can't begin to describe what a relief this was. After all the pain and uncertainty and the endless appointments with doctors, hospitals and specialists, I was finished with them all. I hurried home feeling so pleased with myself and very thankful to Connie for keeping me going through everything.

The weather turned bitterly cold and I hoped for more snow as I couldn't wait to try out the sledge again. I celebrated my certified fitness with a bout of gardening, ably helped by Connie who was kept busy fetching and carrying gardening gloves, knee pads and other paraphernalia. Together we renewed our attack on the brambles that were threatening to crowd out my plants. I puffed and panted as I wielded the mattock. The roots were being particularly stubborn but I was determined not to be defeated.

That evening I felt very stiff, but the doctor had warned me I might still feel some twinges. That was quite normal and nothing to worry about. I'd obviously 'overdone' it, I thought. However, the stiffness persisted and I began to develop pains in my arms. I definitely wasn't improving so I decided to check with my doctor. Driving to my appointment, I noticed that the steering on the car seemed oddly heavy.

'So what have you been up to now?' my GP asked as I slid rather guiltily through his door.

'Just a bit of gardening,' I replied innocently, before admitting to some fairly heavy work. My doctor was reassuring, sure it was just muscle strain. He prescribed some painkillers and told me to return if there was no improvement.

Connie and I went for a walk in Ashdown Forest with my friend Jo. Connie is always wildly excited when she arrives and gives her an especially warm welcome, having never forgotten those early walks when I was immobile in bed. That afternoon I couldn't get rid of the niggling notion that all was not right with me again.

I began having increasingly strange symptoms. The top bolts on the garage doors, usually easy for me to reach, were suddenly inaccessible. When I found a stepladder, I found I could barely climb it. In bed it was difficult to hold my library book, then impossible to turn over easily. I felt heavy and trapped, as if something were pinning me down. My head was like a dead weight that I just could not lift from the pillow and my shoulders, hips and legs all seemed to weigh a ton. As I could no longer sit up unaided in bed, Fred had to help me. This was beyond frustrating and part of me knew there had to be something really wrong.

Reluctantly, I made another doctor's appointment.

Driving for the first time in a week, I found the steering wheel now almost impossibly heavy. I again needed a stick to walk, and when I reached the surgery door I could hardly push it open. Had it always been so difficult? When the doctor sent me for blood tests I had an awful sense of, here we go again . . .

While I was waiting for the test results, my symptoms grew steadily worse. Preparing meals was almost beyond me. I could barely lift the pans, even with two hands, and carrying heavy vegetables, particularly potatoes, was impossible. Connie willingly came to my rescue. She quickly learned to collect potatoes from the pantry in a small bucket, and soon progressed to carrying all the vegetables for me. Before long she fetched a whole range of things from the pantry and brought them to me at the sink. I was thrilled by the speed with which she learned, and as usual she obviously thought this latest game great fun. 'Cooking, Connie! Come and help,' would bring her running to the kitchen. The training we had kept up for interest over the past months was proving an invaluable help to me once again. Connie relished her position as assistant cook, loving the activity but also the close proximity of the goodies pot in the fridge and the fact that I occasionally allowed her to 'help' with some food tasting.

To her delight, I was once more sleeping downstairs in the office-cum-spare bedroom next to the utility room where Connie herself slept. She was thrilled to have my company, which was some comfort as I couldn't believe this was happening to me again, just when I'd thought I was fit and well. I was unable to raise my arms by now so dressing and undressing were a trial, showering was out of the question, washing was difficult and it was back to a plastic bowl on the floor of the bathroom for my feet. Most irritating of all, door knobs were impossible to turn.

It was exhausting trying to force my reluctant limbs to work and I was spending an increasing amount of time resting on my bed. The only problem was that, once there, I was virtually helpless. Connie was wonderful, bringing a rug to cover me and always ready to pick up anything my now feeble hands dropped. I was surprised to find how heavy even a mug of tea had become and how small the handle so that it needed two hands wrapped round the mug to hold it.

When my test results came back they showed I had something called polymyalgic rheumatism. The diagnosis from the doctor was quite alarming – apparently I had a very high blood count, and could have it for about two years. I would be controlled with steroids, and the side effects of taking these would be controlled with further pills to stop me from developing stomach ulcers, and yet more to stop my bones breaking. In addition, I would probably get fat and, the doctor warned, if I failed to take every dose of steroids there was a danger I could go blind! At the time I was weirdly relieved that I had not caused all the strange symptoms myself by working too hard in the wood. Later, I thoroughly alarmed myself by reading the instructions tucked inside one of the boxes of steroids and studying the list of possible side effects. There were so many to choose from, I just hoped I wouldn't get the one where the hair falls out of your head and instead grows abundantly on your face!

The first day I took the steroids, the effect was miraculous. In the morning I simply couldn't move. I was lying propped up in bed, watching Crufts which Fred had thoughtfully recorded for me, when I slipped sideways on my pillows. Fred was out shopping for food and it was impossible for me to get myself back up. I had to wait for him to return and help me. But by four o'clock that afternoon, I was not only able to get myself out of bed, I made tea for us. I found I could easily lift the filled kettle and cups, and also the laden tea tray. For the first few weeks I felt brilliant, physically fit and able to do anything. Friends commented on how well I looked and I realised that my face was starting to appear rather plumper than usual.

After a few weeks, however, I was experiencing quite severe side effects. For the first two hours after I had taken the medication in the morning, I would be wide awake and full of energy. I tried to walk Connie during that time as later the drugs kicked in and I had to sleep, often until late-afternoon. At night I was wide awake again and strangely restless; I'd wander about clearing out drawers and cupboards. I also felt very agitated and, far from piling on fat, I was losing weight fast, but not from my face which grew ever rounder. I was accident-prone, spilling drinks and dropping plates, and I had several painful falls. I also felt quite sick and giddy. Even worse than the physical effects, however, were the mental ones. My moods swung between elation and depression, and I was untypically bad-tempered. I felt confused and could no longer sustain a conversation particularly on the telephone, plus I had memory lapses. It was all very upsetting.

I tried to make the most of the relatively clear-headed hours I had each morning, with sometimes embarrassing consequences. One day I drove into Uckfield, knowing that the children's department in Woolworth's there sold children's T-shirts in my size: boys' age ten. I managed to crash my trolley into a display unit and ram my hip. I was in terrible pain and could not move. The staff wanted to call an ambulance but I eventually managed to walk and went home, giving up on my errand.

The worst episode happened a week later, again in

Woolworth's. I left home early while I was still clear-headed, allowing myself two hours to shop and return before the effects of the drugs began. I was sure all would be well this time but soon after walking into the shop I again crashed my shopping trolley, this time into a stand of rolled-up duvets. I remember watching them fall and roll across the floor as if in slow motion. I was so embarrassed, sure the staff would remember me from the week before. Feeling desperately tired and muddle-headed, I made my way slowly to a café and sat down at a table outside, thinking the fresh air would help to clear my head. I briefly rested it on my hands and woke up an hour later. I don't know what the café owners or people walking past must have thought.

Somehow I managed to get myself home. Not surprisingly, I decided not to drive after this. Some time later, when Fred had driven me to a family lunch and I had staggered both into and out of the pub, without touching a drop of alcohol, I realised that the motion of the car exacerbated the effects of the drugs. I was having regular blood tests and, after a couple of encouraging results, my doctor agreed we could try reducing the dose of steroids slightly, to help with the side effects.

This was probably the hardest time for Connie as she could not understand my abrupt changes of mood. I was having trouble understanding myself at this point. Newfoundlands are very sensitive to noise and when I shouted at her unreasonably for getting in my way as I staggered about she was puzzled. She was as sweet and loyal as always but I would sometimes see her looking at me with a worried expression. Using my walking stick again, I would stumble out to the field to sit in the sunshine on an old chicken crate. Connie always walked by my side and even when I was half-asleep I played games with her.

I used to hide a toy in the crate and she would sniff about until she found its hiding place. However low I was feeling, Connie always made me laugh when we played. I couldn't manage to walk far but it was spring and there was plenty to enjoy at home. The bluebells had carpeted our wood and as they faded were replaced by a blaze of colour from the rhododendrons and azaleas. I watched the great tit parents feed their babies in the old cherry tree until the fledglings were old enough to fly, and to my delight a family of blue tits nested for the first time in years in a bird box in a tall pear tree. Connie carried my cushion when I wanted to sit on the patio. It's such a peaceful, almost secret place, screened by banks of billowing flowers in summer, perfect for when I needed to rest, listening to the bird song and bees humming. Connie seemed to like lying there, too, but at a movement from me she was instantly awake. Without a word from me she would carefully pick up my cushion and follow me back indoors.

As the steroids were reduced, I gradually improved over the summer until I felt much more like myself. I had the incentive of the Newfoundland Water Trials in July to spur me on as well as another companion dog show and obedience competition in a neighbouring village. There were always new things to teach Connie for, with my recent record, who knew what might go wrong with me next!

When putting my wellington boots on, in my fuddled state, I would keep knocking them over, so the first job was to teach Connie to stand them up for me. 'Pick up, Connie,' I would nudge the top edge of the boot to get her interest at the same time. She carefully gripped the edge and stood it up, brilliant. That was all I needed her to do at first. The next step was to bring me one boot. The really hard part that she learnt later was to pick up two boots at the same time. She found it very hard to

131

grasp two boots as one would keep falling over. I realised I could make it easier by standing them beside a stool in the hall with an old flat iron on the other side, and then they didn't fall over. She then found it difficult again. I couldn't understand it, but when I looked carefully I saw it was my fault. I had tidily pushed the boots so far back she could not get her head in the right position to get hold of them, much to her frustration. A lesson we should all remember is that if a dog cannot do something it is nearly always our fault.

13

Water Trials and Training

It had always been my plan to enter Connie for the Newfoundland Water Trials that year, as I had with Cassie and Christie in the past, although because of my illness we had managed virtually no practice. I was still absolutely determined to enter, though, and so that summer we began a crash course in preparation for the trials at the end of July. A major part is the retrieve, and to train for this I began by practising on land using a water toy before progressing to the water itself. Connie had to learn to sit and stay while I threw the toy. She was then sent to fetch it and as soon as she had the toy, I would call and give hand signals so that she would know exactly where to bring it out. On reaching the bank, I'd say, 'Hold,' then 'Give,' training her to hold on to the toy until I had it. The next command would be, 'Shake.' If the commands are not given in this order, dogs tend to shake and drop the toy or other item back into the water where you cannot reach it or into an equally inconvenient patch of nettles on the bank.

Teaching a dog to tow a boat to shore, which is another part of the trials, requires a different technique. Usually in training a dog is taught to fetch an item, return it to its owner and gently 'Give', all of which Connie could perform perfectly. However, to tow a boat, she needed to learn to grip a boat's fender attached to a rope and 'Pull' as she moved away from me. I tried this first indoors, then outside in the garden just using a fender and rope. The next vital step is to attach the rope to a boat. For this I needed Fred's help. He had to hold on to Connie on the bank while I rowed away shouting and splashing the oars to keep her excited and interested. Just as he had previously with Cassie and Christie, Fred held Connie back until the moment when I called and he sent her out to the boat. That first time we tried it on water, all the while as Connie swam, I kept calling her. The land training worked. Connie swam straight to the boat, gripped the fender and towed me back to shore, holding on until Fred had taken the rope from her.

The last thing to practise was a little more complicated. The Water Trials were being held on 28 July, which was fast approaching, and so far Connie had done almost no training on water besides towing the boat. With my reduced level of medication I was at last safe to drive again so Connie and I set off to visit Derek and Stella. It was my intention that my sister-in-law and I would both take Connie into the sea to practise retrieving from the water and, most importantly, 'rescuing a drowning stranger'.

When we left home the weather was perfect, warm and sunny with barely a breath of wind. By the time we arrived at the coast it did not feel quite so warm, the sun had vanished behind a cloud and a rather brisk breeze was blowing. Not easily discouraged, Stella and I changed into swimming costumes and I added a life jacket. We walked to the sea front bundled up in thick sweaters and warm trousers over our swimwear. I had made it absolutely clear to Stella that I was definitely going to swim, whatever. The grey and rather sullen sea that faced me did not match the inviting blue I had imagined, though. Reluctantly, I pulled off my sweater. My skin immediately broke into goose bumps as a decidedly fresh sea wind buffeted it. I dipped one shrinking toe into a wave as it lapped the shore, and jumped back. The water was freezing. No way was I going in.

Stella, her back to the sea, laughed and called me chicken. She was still laughing when a huge wave sneaked up and soaked her. Realising it made no difference as she was already wet, she bravely plunged into the next one. Well, she had worked as a PE teacher for years. Giving me up as a lost cause, she called heartily back to Connie, to encourage her in. It suddenly seemed very important that I should remain on the beach to direct and guide my dog, while Stella did the swimming. As it worked out, she was the only one who really swam that day because Connie made a half-hearted attempt but quickly decided the waves were too dangerous and we walked on the beach instead.

Luckily, that day at the beach was not our only chance to practise. We were fortunate enough to have the use of a private lake close to home, and once again I had someone else to brace the cold water instead of me. Our son Michael, another hardy PE teacher, was very happy to don his wetsuit and dive into the lake. David, Nathalie, Tom and Lili came along to watch and encourage. The first attempt was a big success. Connie successfully rescued them both. The second was less encouraging as she abandoned the 'rescue' and left them to drown! I solved the problem by throwing her favourite toy to the drowning son, encouraging Connie to swim out and tow him back as she was keen to save her toy.

I was allotted the extremely important job of rowing out into the lake, calling to Connie and encouraging her to pull the boat back to shore. This suited me very well as it had the great advantage of keeping me quite dry and warm. It is an amazing feeling to sit in a boat while it is being pulled along by a dog. At one point I gave up the boat to the children who, bored with simply watching, had great fun practising their rowing skills, safely beached on dry land, while their father and uncle once more braved the cold for more rescue work.

I couldn't help but remember similar days when the boys were younger. Cassie and Christie had both loved the water and the boys used to play rescue games with them. Barry, Michael and David all learned to row on the pond in our wood when they were quite young. Wearing life jackets, they were quite safe but could still feel intrepid. Cassie in particular used to 'rescue' Michael from his dinghy. She probably had the strongest water instincts of all my Newfoundlands. From the very beginning, I would find her frantically 'digging' in her water bowl, just as Connie did when she first arrived.

One holiday we visited the Lake District with the boys and allowed Michael to row his dinghy out on a lake. I remained watching from the shore with David, who was just a toddler at the time, and Cassie. I didn't really notice but Cassie obviously became increasingly worried. She had been taught to rescue people from water and pull boats back to the shore. Now here she was, stranded on the beach, while her beloved Michael headed out into the middle of a vast expanse of water. Every instinct urged her to rescue him and so she slipped away from me and swam out to Michael. She was desperate to rescue him, although he was obviously fully in control and quite happy. When she reached his dinghy, however, there was no pull rope for her to hold on to while dragging him back to shore. Intent on her rescue, she instead grabbed one of the oars and tried swimming with that, the problem being that this spun the boat round the wrong way. Not to be deterred, she swam round to the other oar and tried pulling that for a while, until the same thing happened. Cassie spent ages swimming with first one oar and then the other, so keen was she to return Michael safely to me on the shore. We still have that pair of oars as a memento, with Cassie's teeth marks etched upon them.

We often went for day trips to Pevensey, our nearest seaside location, where Cassie could practise her water work. I would swim out while Fred held Cassie back on the beach. Again, she would be so frantic to get to me out of the water that Fred would have to lash her to the breakwater until I was sufficiently far out and could signal him to send her to me. As soon as she was released, Cassie would plunge into the sea and swim out to join me, waiting for me to grab hold of her shoulder or fur, at which point she would swim back to shore dragging me along. It was the most wonderful sensation.

We also spent many happy times in the summer splashing about in the sea while staying at my mother's house near Bognor, with first Cassie, then Eliza and Christie – though Eliza was always careful to stay well away from the shore, digging in the dry sand instead.

Fred and I had loved boats and the water since we were children and eventually, having hired for years, we bought our own boat on the Norfolk Broads where the boys all learned to sail. Barry was so keen that he also bought a small boat and at one time, when David was still young enough to be bossed around and not old enough to protest loudly enough, Barry used to throw him overboard so as to practise his own water rescue skills. No one came to any harm and I think David secretly enjoyed playing his role of 'drowning' victim.

Christie's water instincts were put to practical use closer

to home in October 2000. I looked outside as I always do first thing in the morning and saw that the lane appeared to be moving. A closer inspection showed that it was flooded as were most of the lanes and fields around Uckfield and Lewes. In Uckfield, the town shops were under water and there were lifeboats in the high street. Venturing out, we came across a stranded airline pilot wading along the lanes still dressed in his smart uniform. We also tried to rescue a waterlogged sheep from the field. We managed to settle her in front of the Aga where she was at least warm and comfortable. Christie and Eliza watched quietly, seeming to understand, but sadly the sheep died.

Christie found the flood water running everywhere quite normal and great fun, happily retrieving dropped keys from beneath it, unlike Eliza. On our usual walks, if you wanted to keep your feet dry, you just had to follow Eliza's path – she had an unerring instinct for dry land. With everywhere flooded there were of course no dry paths and so I carried her. From her lofty perch Eliza enjoyed the novel watery smells without getting her paws wet. The only time she was ever happy to go near water was when the fur on her tummy was muddy whereupon she voluntarily went to the kitchen sink to be washed.

I had not been to the Newfoundland Water Trials for years, not since I'd last entered with Christie in the early-90s, taking Michael and David with me. This time, Fred and I towed our caravan to a farm site near Bideford on Avon, close to where we had first met all those years ago at the gliding club. It was not long after there had been serious floods in the area, and walking Connie near the river, it was still obvious just how high the water levels had been, with tidemarks on hedges and trees where the floodwater had rushed through. Shops in the village were still shut and signs of the devastation were all too clear, reminding me of the mess left behind by our local floods.

Although the tests at the trials were essentially the same, the way they were performed had been totally changed, mainly due to the dreaded Health and Safety regulations, which seem to affect every aspect of life which might actually be fun, as well as insurance problems. There are various events – Puppy and Veteran swim, Beginners and Advanced Water Trials, Beginners and Open Obedience, and Working and Decorated Carts. I had decided to enter Connie for the Open Obedience and Beginners Water Trial for which she would have to swim thirty yards out to a boat and then tow it to shore, retrieve a floating object, and finally rescue a 'drowning stranger' for full marks, or her owner for half marks. I'd opted for the stranger. It was only as we were about to start that I discovered that, thanks to revised regulations, the boat Connie would have to tow back to shore was huge and very heavy, and now paddled by two men. She also had to be sent out to the boat from the water rather than the bank and there was no fender on the rope for her to pull on.

My heart sank as I set out from the shore with the two rowers. Connie had not had very much practice and everything was so different, I really did not think she would manage. It was also a far longer swim out than she was used to. Determined to make the best of it, though, I called to her excitedly. To my amazement she kept on swimming right up to the boat, where she grabbed the rope and efficiently towed a heavy boat, two grown men and one very proud owner back to the bank. Connie then successfully completed her water retrieve and finally attempted to rescue the drowning stranger. She swam close, took a very good long look, then turned for the shore, leaving the stranger to drown! Unsurprisingly, she was unplaced in the event but she had worked so well, given her curtailed training. It was then time for the obedience class, and to my complete surprise Connie won. I was thrilled because Cassie had also won the same obedience class three years running and I now have a silver cup showing both her name and dates and Connie's.

Alongside the water work and excitement of the trials, life at home continued as usual. Although I was so much fitter by the summer, Connie continued as my willing assistant, continually learning new skills as well as refining and polishing everything she already knew. For the second year running, I had missed out on so much earlier in the year while I was ill that it was lovely to be able to visit friends and family and go for long walks once more.

At home I had a little basket that would just hold half a dozen eggs. I wondered if Connie could carry that without breaking them. She could! It was lovely to see one hundred pounds of Newfoundland carefully carrying the eggs to the sink.

I decided to teach her to close the door of the cupboard next to the tumble dryer. She quickly learned the new command 'Shut the door', and we gradually built up the exercise until Connie took the detergent ball out of the washing machine, placed it back in the cupboard and then shut the door. She completed her tasks so enthusiastically, knowing there was a treat waiting by the end, that sometimes she shut the door with such gusto it would fly open again. 'Gently, gently,' said in a calm voice, would encourage her to give several tiny pushes with her nose until the door was properly shut.

I wondered whether she could manage to open a cupboard door since she had learned to close on. This proved more tricky as I did not really want Connie holding the door knob with her teeth. I solved the problem by looping a short length of dog lead around the handle for her to pull on. I also realised that when we open a door we can simply bend our arm, but Connie would actually need to back away while holding the lead then stop once the door was opened, quite a complex operation. The first part was easy as she knew the command 'Hold', and I managed to teach her the next part of backing up while holding the lead by moving a treat backwards, all the time reminding her to hold. Eyes keenly fixed on the treat, Connie took a few steps back. She was then very happy to drop the lead and eat up the piece of chicken as reward.

As mentioned earlier, Crispin had always helped me when I was gardening by pulling up any weeds that were particularly well rooted and, remembering this, I encouraged Connie to do the same. She would tug at a weed with gusto, knowing she was allowed to play with it afterwards, tossing it about, shaking it, and generally making a game for herself.

By the time she was two, Connie understood a wide range of commands which I had begun using when she was just a small puppy. I started with a few simple verbal commands, always accompanied by hand signals and clear body language.

Some useful commands which I use most days:

The first one is 'Come'. I call, 'Connie, come!' which always means there is something nice for her when she comes to me; and 'Connie?' as a question, which usually means there is some interesting work for her to do.

'Leave' is said firmly. And if I say it firmly but quietly Connie knows it means do not pick up or chase something. It means leave the treat until I say she can eat it.

'Pick up' is said in a high, happy voice.

When I want Connie to hold something, I say 'Hold' gently but firmly, and if we are going to walk somewhere with it, I say 'Carry' in a light happy voice.

When I want Connie to give me something, I say 'Give', and add, 'Good girl' when she gives it to me.

I use the word 'Drop' in slightly different ways. If something is not suitable or disgusting I say it briskly, but if I want Connie to carefully lower, for instance, a bucket of potatoes, I then say 'Drop' slowly, and as she carefully puts it down I gradually lower her treat to the floor.

'Seek' means 'Use your nose', usually accompanied by offering Connie my hand to sniff, which means she then rushes off round the field to follow the scent and retrieve my glove or whatever it is that I've dropped. This is always said in an upbeat, happy way.

'Find' is similar but often used for things I have thrown or dropped in undergrowth for her to find, and again this is said in a high, happy voice to suggest it's exciting and she should use eyes and nose.

'Fetch' I use mainly for obedience training. It basically means to go and fetch an item, bring it to me and sit holding it until I tell her to give it to me. Again this is said briskly but happily.

'Steady' is said slowly but firmly and serves as a warning. It means to go carefully, or if we are going down a steep hill it tells Connie to walk on a loose lead beside me; it's just a 'be careful' command rather than tight heel work.

'No' means that Connie has not yet found what I wanted so she should keep looking. It is not said crossly. I use the word 'Leave' if she is about to pick up something she should not, and that would be said more briskly and crossly. I use, 'No . . . no . . . no . . . yes!' when training and Connie is looking for something as you would in a game of Hunt the Thimble to suggest the seeker is getting warmer. Or, if she is heading for my gloves and I want her to bring my socks, I will say 'No' and point to what I really want. Or when she is tracking, if I need her to go back and find something, I will encourage her with a wave of my arms.

'Yes' is said encouragingly and in a high voice, often followed by 'Good girl'. Dogs love praise words, especially 'Yes' and 'What a good girl/ dog'.

For praise generally I use a high voice accompanied by clapping and a big smile. This is always done immediately. When Connie gets something right I usually laugh and offer her a titbit and a big cuddle so she knows immediately and learns. I've found the quicker the reward is offered, the quicker the dog learns.

At first all commands are very short and clear. I use my voice, hand signals and body language, and as time goes by my signals and commands become more refined and subtle. Hardly any commands are needed with Connie now – she just knows what I want.

I'm constantly building on and adding to these commands but they form the basis of all the work and training I have done with Connie, and with my other dogs in the past. It's obviously vital to be consistent and to decide what works for you in establishing a good rapport with your dog so that you both clearly understand one another. Many of the problems I've seen in my behavioural work come about simply because the dog just does not understand what is expected or gets mixed messages from his owner.

14

Celebrity Dog

September brought warm autumn sunshine and masses of ripe blackberries. I love blackberrying as it always reminds me of my childhood excursions, followed by a flurry of pie- and jam-making and the delicious smell of cooking fruit. Connie enjoys helping, carefully eating all the low-hanging berries from the field hedges. When I kept bantams there was one particularly sweet-natured cockerel that would flutter up to peck a ripe blackberry which he then unselfishly offered to his hen to enjoy. Foxes often appear to feast on the juicy dark berries, as do flocks of birds, but one day I was amazed to see a rabbit which had somehow climbed on to the bench by the hedge and was stretching up to reach the berries with its paws delicately balanced on the arm rest.

If I pick up the tea tray and head for the door, Connie knows at once that I am going to sit outside. Without a word from me, she searches around for my cushion and follows me out. One day she obviously couldn't find the usual cushion, so improvised by bringing her own fluffy bed for me to sit on. I have only to say, 'Rug, Connie,' and she will go back to the house to fetch it for me. It is always neatly gathered up as she does not like anything to drag on the ground. I am completely spoilt as she will also find my sun hat, and will carefully position the cushion exactly where I want it on the bench.

After one rather lazy day in early-October I remembered that the *Argus* newspaper, which had run the article about Connie over a year ago, had asked me to get in touch with an update. When I telephoned they were again extremely interested and sent over a photographer to take more photographs that very afternoon. As usual this prompted a flurry of manic activity from me – grooming a Newfoundland and then keeping her clean and tidy is something of a nightmare when her natural element is water, mud and a tangle of brambles. Then there was the house which normally has a fair scattering of dog hairs, leaves, and a certain amount of mud on the floors and sometimes up the walls, too ... and that was before I'd done anything about my own appearance, which was vital considering my usual attire was tatty trousers, worn with an elderly sweater and no make-up. Lastly, just before the photographer arrived, I needed to collect Connie's props including baskets and buckets of vegetables, ready for her to be photographed in action.

Shooting just a few photographs can mean anything from one to two hours' hard work for Connie. She is such a good-natured dog that she will happily pose for shot after shot, changing position, fetching and carrying, exactly where and when I say. That afternoon the photographer was particularly keen to capture her with her basket of eggs. She was used to carrying them from the pantry to the kitchen but he wanted to show her carrying them up the drive, with the eggs piled high in the basket to make them clearly visible. This meant they could easily fall out and, to take the best angle, the photographer was lying down at the top of the drive. Connie's natural response to someone lying in front of her would be to jump on them enthusiastically, so I could foresee a few problems. In the event she behaved perfectly and all the effort seemed worthwhile when I saw the photo of her holding her basket of eggs on the front page of the *Argus* again.

Even more exciting and unexpected was being filmed for the television news. I'm so used to my family being fairly blasé and taking everything Connie does for granted that it's surprising to me just how fascinated other people are by her. I had just finished the weekly supermarket shop and was sitting in the hairdresser's when I got a call from Fred saying there was a TV news crew waiting at our gate, wanting to film Connie for the BBC South East regional news programme that very night. I could hardly believe it. They had seen the article in the *Argus* and wanted to run their own feature. Luckily when I got home, dressed in my usual scruffy best, the crew were away eating lunch at the local pub so I could slink indoors and change into something more suitable. Should I attempt some miraculous transformation into a TV star? I decided on balance probably not, but at least my hair was looking good after the hairdresser's attentions. I refused to let the crew in for another twenty minutes, which was hardly long enough for me to get everything ready but I quickly changed and it gave me a moment to brush and groom Connie, who having spent a very boring morning was exceptionally bouncy.

When the film crew reappeared, she was beside herself with excitement at the buzz of activity and all the new people to meet. She was also fascinated by the huge camera. This is going to be a fiasco, I thought, mentally preparing myself to look foolish, but again Connie was amazing. As soon as we began filming she transformed herself from wild thing to sensible working dog. I was, as always, so impressed by her. She had to carry her bucket of food from the pantry to the sink, over and over again, and not once did she try to eat any of it. She also accepted the cameraman hiding at the back of the pantry to film her as if it was a normal everyday occurrence. It took well over two hours to film what ended up as a one-and-a-half minute slot on the television, and when it was over I was shattered. Connie must also have been very tired but she was still determined to help carry in my shopping which had been forgotten in all the excitement. Just a few short hours later it was thrilling for us to watch her at work on the television news.

The next day I was called up to talk on a Scottish radio news and current affairs programme. This was another exciting first for me but at least it didn't require any effort from Connie. I enjoyed myself. I'm always happy to talk about Connie and the training we have done together, and it was the perfect opportunity to highlight just how capable dogs really are.

Shortly after this, I had a rather more local event looming which was filling me with dread. In the summer, Connie had won an obedience class at a neighbouring village show and, in the giddy flush of success, I'd recklessly agreed to give a talk and demonstration on how I trained her to a nearby obedience club. To make matters worse, this was the club to which my dear friend Sas and Connie's great friend Oliver belonged, which would make it even more embarrassing if we made a mess of things.

When the day arrived the butterflies in my stomach were in full frantic flight. Sas came early to support me but left Oliver behind at home. We both knew the temptation for the dogs to play madly would be too great if they were at the meeting together. Bringing back uncomfortable memories of our first ring-craft class, Connie barged ahead when we entered the hall. Pulling me behind at an undignified scramble, she lunged excitedly at any new arrivals, keen to give them a warm welcome. When I peeped into the room where I was to give my talk and demonstration, my heart sank. Inviting plates of food, including Connie's favourite cheese, were set out on low tables, easily within her reach – and I'd planned for her to be off her lead for most of the practical demonstration.

I led Connie, sniffing appreciatively, over to my seat as the club members took theirs. Connie lay down as instructed and, luckily for me, the preliminary meeting went on just long enough for her to calm down and even have a snooze. When my big moment came, for a few seconds I was completely speechless – not something that often happens to me. I began hesitantly but rapidly gained confidence as I spoke about Connie. When she was called upon she went through her repertoire faultlessly, performing everything I asked, including her latest party piece which was to take my handkerchief from my pocket when I sneezed – silly, I know, but it made everyone laugh. Connie worked between the rows of people, off the lead, totally ignoring the plates of food within easy reach. I was so proud!

Life returned to normal, with the usual hectic preparations for a big family Christmas, and almost before I realised it we had reached New Year. For the last two years I'd started out with such high hopes and been forced to put my plans on hold so this year I felt a certain amount of trepidation. Again events took a surprising turn, but this year in a good way.

Early on 3 January I was woken abruptly by the telephone. Not properly awake, I had to ask the caller to repeat twice that they were Southern Counties Radio calling for Hazel Carter. 'We've seen Connie's story in the *Daily Mail* and want to interview you.' Somewhat bemused, I gave my first interview of the day, glad it was over the telephone and they could not see my dishevelled appearance. I'd had no idea that the story was even being run in the *Daily Mail* but went on to give four more radio interviews that day. The phone rang constantly – who would have guessed an article in a national newspaper would generate such a frenzy of interest? Fred spent the rest of the day in our bedroom fielding non-stop telephone calls while Connie and I were filmed for television downstairs.

In the morning it was a crew from ITV regional news. I really loved this session. Two delightful chaps came to interview me and film Connie. We laughed so much that we had to keep reshooting. At one point Connie had to sit close to the producer, holding my rug in her mouth while he talked to camera. I had to position her and at the same time hold the sound mic over his head. The producer would get partway through, forget his lines and have to start again. This happened so many times that by the end we were all helpless with laughter. Connie patiently took the rug again and again but was obviously just a little bored as on the last take she tossed her head impatiently as though to say, Oh, do come on! We have a DVD recording of the programme and every time I see her shake her head it makes me smile.

That afternoon, an American television company arrived to film us. It was very strange to think that Connie's image and story would be broadcast on both sides of the Atlantic. I have never seen so many people packed into our small cottage. As well as the film crew there were various extras all interested in watching, from the taxi driver to the producer's daughter who was longing to play with Connie. Everywhere I turned there were people, along with sound recording equipment, video cameras, and cables snaking perilously just where I might step and trip. Connie was very excited when they first appeared but soon settled down. She was fast becoming a pro! However, I quickly realised that she was not paying as much attention to me as usual. In fact, she seemed fixated on the crew's bags which had been left on the kitchen floor. She kept returning to them, head down, snuffling. It was only then I thought to ask what was actually inside. 'Oh, just our lunch and some sausage rolls,' the producer replied casually.

We moved the bags and Connie began concentrating on the work in hand. This was the hardest part to film for me as I had to remember to work to camera and talk to the producer, who was appearing on the programme alongside me, while giving Connie all her signals at the same time. Juggling it all was extremely difficult and needed lots of concentration but Connie was completely unfazed and performed perfectly. She gives me such confidence that, whatever happens, I know she will always be there, ready to help me.

I needed all the confidence I could muster for our next venture into the spotlight. One of the many phone calls that had poured in after the *Daily Mail* article was an invitation to appear on the ITV programme *This Morning Live*. I'd agreed, then started to worry. All the filming and photography so far had taken place in the security of our own home; for this Connie and I would have to go into the television studio.

Barry had kindly offered to drive us there and stay to help me with Connie. We still needed to get up at 4.30 in the morning to arrive in time, and I'd spent most of the previous day ensuring Connie's coat was gleaming after an intensive bathing and grooming session. I'd then had to keep her clean, not easy when she had to perform her toilet in a muddy field. Newfoundlands are skilled at getting themselves and their owners filthy in seconds. We managed, however, and arrived at the studio in good order, where Connie took her first-ever ride in a lift.

We were met by the producer who explained exactly what would happen. As well as a short chat, there was to be a demonstration showing a little of what Connie could do. But she was not the only animal on the programme that morning, apparently. There would also be pigs, which made me feel rather uneasy. Although Connie is a country dog and completely familiar with horses, sheep and cattle, and even the odd llama, she had never before encountered a pig. It seemed a sensible idea to introduce her before the show started so we took Connie along to the pigs' room where several tame miniature piglets were happily grunting and squealing in a cage.

Barry stayed with Connie and the pigs while I went off to be professionally made up ready for filming. I'd never been professionally made up before and was thrilled. I asked the make-up artist if she could make the bags under my eyes disappear and she did a fantastic job. My face was so improved, I carefully kept the make-up on for the next twenty-four hours (not, I am reliably told, what you are supposed to do)! The producer came to see me just as I finished in make-up to break the news that the piglets would now be on set at the same time as Connie. I would have turned white with worry if it had not been for the rosy blusher.

There was no need for concern. By the time I found Barry and Connie, still with the pigs, Connie had a new friend. She was rubbing noses with one of the piglets, now wearing a harness and lead. They were soon together on the set like familiar old chums, Connie sitting angelically while the piglets were fed and petted close by.

Our moment of fame was very short as the programme ran out of time but everything went like clockwork. The only slight hitch came a little later when we were leaving. The lift we had used earlier was not working so we had to use the stairs. Our visit to David's flat should have warned me this would be a problem. Now, at the studio, Connie steadfastly refused to move. At one point I thought we might just have to wait for the lift to be fixed. It took all Barry's and my powers of persuasion plus the attention of a host of TV celebs to encourage her to budge, but eventually, very reluctantly she managed to make it downstairs.

Connie's brush with fame was not quite over. A few weeks later it was a great surprise to hear that she and I had been nominated among the five pairs of finalists in the Friends For Life event at Crufts. Connie does go to dog shows, but is not a top show dog as she is rather small for her breed. I knew it was unlikely we would ever get to Crufts by doing well at championship shows. But now Connie, my home help and country dog, was going to appear in a starring role in the biggest dog show in the world – how exciting!

Once again we had a film crew with us. Connie was well used to this by now. She worked for five hours with only short breaks while they filmed her pulling up weeds, bringing the shopping in and helping me indoors, even doing the washing which is always popular. The finished film would only run for about a minute, after all that work!

My husband and I – and Connie, of course – were to be treated like royalty with free accommodation in a most beautiful hotel on the site of the National Exhibition Centre, Birmingham, where Crufts was held, and free passes for the show.

I had no idea what to wear. In a panic I rushed off to the shops, looking for something suitably smart for the occasion. The outfit needed to be a light colour, to show

153

off Connie's black fur. I quickly discovered I must be a skinny midget – nothing was small enough for me. In desperation I dragged out an old suit from the depths of our bedroom cupboard. The next problem was wondering if Connie would find a suitable place for her toilet while we were away, as she is used to the privacy of our field. I also worried about how she would cope with the huge crowds and all the noise at Crufts. Our event was to be broadcast on TV and would also be shown live on all the screens in the exhibitors' halls. The very thought of my dog panicking in those circumstances, or simply galloping off around the arena with me trying to hang on, was unnerving.

The five finalists all stayed at the hotel together and all got on so well. We finished up like old friends. Also staying there were the winners and their dogs from the two previous years so it was lovely getting to know them as well. Connie also enjoyed making new canine friends, especially a very sweet German Shepherd bitch who was one of her fellow finalists. We had a rehearsal on Saturday night in the huge arena, which was great fun. On the Sunday morning there was time for me to take Connie all round Crufts. She just loved all the crowds and attention as people recognised her from television. She was like a film star, posing for many photo sessions and happily wagging her tail for all the children and grown ups who wanted to make a fuss of her.

On Sunday night before the big event we were treated to a delicious buffet supper and the dogs were invited too. It was a super party which we all enjoyed, but as the time approached for us to go down to the arena I think several of us were getting a little nervous. The owner of Sadie, the German Shepherd, was worried that she might be upset by all the noise in the arena as she had rescued her from a terrible past. I suggested that Connie should go first and Sadie could follow her New Best Friend.

The climax of the weekend arrived and there we were, with all the lights, music, commentary and six thousand people watching and clapping. Our dogs were very well behaved and quite calm. We were all presented with our finalists' awards. Then came the big moment when they announced the overall winner. We were all very pleased that Harriet Ringsell, a young girl in a wheelchair, won it with her Hungarian Vizsla, Yepa. It was justly deserved in every way.

The TV coverage only showed a very small part of Friends For Life, but we have all been sent a copy on DVD so that we can enjoy watching it and remember our wonderful celebrity weekend.

The excitement over, it was time to return to our real life, although during the next weeks I was very moved by all the letters and messages I received from people who had seen us, telling me how inspired they were by Connie's story.

At home again we fell comfortably back into our quiet daily routine. Typically we would begin the day with a walk, with me dropping my keys 'accidentally' somewhere near the gate for Connie to find. I marvel at how adept she has become at this. Often there is washing to do. I have got into the habit of throwing everything down the stairs into the hall and Connie fetches bundle after bundle which she drops into the wash box as I begin loading the washing machine. If the floor needs sweeping, which it invariably does (the downside of my large furry companion), I will shake the dusty door mat outside and leave it there while I carry on sweeping. Connie lies outside while I am busy but at a word from me, picks up a corner of the heavy mat and drags it back inside, positioning it carefully by the door.

Later when the washing cycle is finished Connie helps again. I open the machine door and say simply, 'Washing machine, tumble dryer.' I can sit lazily watching as Connie goes back and forth emptying the washer and loading the dryer. She bangs the door shut, then picks up the detergent ball and returns it to the cupboard. When the clothes are dry Connie will take them out and place them in the laundry basket for me. She is so familiar with all these laundry tasks that they are completed with hardly a word from me.

Connie also comes along when I go shopping as there is a conveniently shady spot behind the Co-op to park. Back home, she helps bring in the shopping. She has progressed from using her wicker basket to efficiently carrying the plastic carrier bags and if there is a chicken to go into the cellar freezer, Connie sits patiently at the top of the steep stairs holding the chicken in its bag while I climb down the first few steps. With only a look from me, she leans forward carefully to pass the bag to me. On another day when I want to cook the chicken, she will take it back from me as I climb up the cellar stairs.

After lunch, with the household tasks finished, we might work in the wood. Connie helps me by pulling out young saplings. 'Pull, pull,' I say and she tugs hard on the roots until they give way. I usually hide one of my gloves for her to find, snuffling and pawing at the ground until she discovers it beneath a pile of leaves. Afterwards she is covered with leaves and needs brushing. I begin with the brush and when I need the comb all I have to say is, 'Comb, Connie' and she picks it up and passes it to me. She will also find the brush if I ask. At one time, Connie fidgeted and grew bored as it takes such a time to groom her dense coat but these days she loves it because she knows there will be treats when she passes me the brush and comb.

Preparing for the evening meal, I stand by the worktop while Connie brings me all the ingredients. If I have forgotten to close the pantry door all I need to do is look at it and Connie, noticing my glance, instantly rushes to shut the door for me. Needless to say there is always some tasty piece of meat as a reward. At dinner time if Fred is in the sitting-room, perhaps chatting with our youngest son David, Connie will take a large cupboard notice with 'Dinner is waiting' written on it to summon them. After supper she carries the little basket with chocolate bars inside for us and then contentedly curls up close to the fire for the evening, dozing and half listening to the buzz of chatter, happy with her day's activities.

It is now early-March, a still and frosty morning. The fluffy long-tailed tits have come early for their breakfast today. Connie helps by eating a couple of crumbs, just to check my culinary skills, before I feed them. This is our first job of the day, before we have a quick breakfast. 'Socks,' I call then, and she rushes off to find them. 'Boots,' I say, opening the hall door. 'Two boots,' I remind her cautiously as she rushes through excitedly. Back she proudly comes with both boots firmly clasped at the top edge. After all this time there is not a tooth mark on them. She knows as soon as she has brought them that we are off on our first walk of the day, and this is her reward for smartly fetching them.

There's a refreshing ice-cold nip in the air to wake us up as we step outside after the warmth of the Aga in the kitchen. We set off down the woodland gully, over the bridge and up the other side to our boundary and the stile. I climb over it easily today. It is still shady here at the bottom of the big field. Tantalisingly, I can see the sun shining at the top of the hill. Connie is enjoying herself, investigating the many interesting scents of fox and badger. She particularly loves rabbits, and especially the droppings that she hoovers up eagerly, forgetting she has just had her breakfast. I can see fresh deer prints etched sharply through the frosty turf. Higher up the hill we will probably see the deer themselves before they melt mysteriously away through the thicket of dark trees bordering the field.

We reach the top of the hill. What a beautiful day it is. The sky, a perfect pale blue, is silent and still except for the birds that are just waking up. I look towards the south-west, across unspoiled countryside, to the distant hazy lines of the South Downs. Turning round, I gaze back over the peaceful valley to our cottage, shadowy beneath the trees. Beyond, rising on the other side, is a patchwork of little fields, the early sun highlighting the occasional farm or cottage, the hedges and the grazing sheep. I bend down and stroke Connie's fluffy black head. 'Come on, Connie. Time to go.'

We go back to our wood, the sun now filtering through the bare branches of the trees. I sit in a patch of sunshine on an old rustic seat by the bridge and think about my life with Connie. She is now two and a half – what a lot we have done together already. How I worried about her while I was immobile, and how she inspired me and made me even more determined to get fit so we could enjoy life together. She has always loved her 'work'. Even as a tiny puppy she really enjoyed fetching and carrying things, always believing I was thinking up wonderful interesting new games for her!

What fun we have both had, and how much we have achieved. Ironically, if I had not had these health problems, I'm sure I would not have trained her to do so many things. I believe that she is unique in the diverse range of activities she can carry out. If I had been fit I would have been out and about more, rushing around, thinking of other things. But lying in bed, waiting for the painkillers to work, or sitting feeling sick and giddy, gave me all the time I needed to work out exactly how to train her, within my limitations. I am convinced that my having to be at home so much helped develop the very special bond between us, though she has always been sweet-tempered, gentle and extremely adaptable. I'm still amazed by her ability to understand any new task so quickly. Ever-observant, she is always watching me, ready for the smallest signal from me to carry out a request.

Now here I am, Connie snoozing beside me, perhaps dreaming of her walks in Ashdown Forest or visits to the seaside. Early primroses are peeping shyly through the tangled grass in this sheltered spot by the bridge; around my feet shoots of bright green bluebells are appearing through last year's fallen leaves. Soon the wood will be covered in a scented blue sea. It was well worth all the enjoyable work through the winter months, clearing away the brambles and dead bracken.

This is the life that I love, spent peacefully here at home in the woods and fields with Connie, my husband and visiting family. There has been a lot of publicity because of the work Connie does, which both of us have really enjoyed, and it has been wonderful meeting so many new people. it has been lovely to hear how many others have now been inspired by what Connie and I have achieved, as that has always been very important to me. If I can encourage people, make them feel confident, lift their depression so they feel happy and motivated, I shall be very pleased – especially if, like me, they are older or have disabilities or medical problems. Hopefully their dogs will now be able to stay with the people they know and love instead of being re-homed.

'What shall we do this year, Connie?' I ask. She stretches luxuriously after her rest and looks up at me with her soft brown eyes and questioning expression. Spring is here, my favourite time of year. 'We can do more water work. We must swim together again, and you can pull me along and practise towing the boat.' She looks interested by my suggestions and stands up, waiting expectantly. 'Come on, Connie, time for work. It's getting really warm now . . . can you carry my coat?'

15

And Finally . . .

This book has obviously been about my lovely Connie, what we have achieved so far and our life together. But none of this would have been possible without all the other dogs I have known over the years, and in particular my own wonderful dogs who have inspired and encouraged me through the best and worst of times. All very different and individual in character, the devotion and companionship of each has meant so much to me. Without them, my life would have been much less rich and colourful.

Freckles
He was a roan Cocker Spaniel and my grandmother's dog. He was my inspiration and from him I learned the first important lesson in dog behavioural work – rewards work! He steadfastly refused to let me take him for a walk further than the garden boundary – until, that is, I raided the dog biscuit tin and laid a tempting trail for him through the garden gate and into the lane. He used to meet my grandmother from the bus, and closed the door for her if there was a draught.

Sandy

1949–59. Another Cocker Spaniel, though golden-red this time. My first dog, how could I forget him? From difficult beginnings he became a true companion, running alongside when I was out riding and, like Freckles before him with my grandmother, meeting me from my school bus. He loved holidays and often came with us on my first boating holidays on the Norfolk Broads.

Crispin

1965–79. He was a handsome, dark gold-coloured Golden Retriever. He went everywhere with me, from work to the bank, shops and restaurants. He was my first dog as an adult and I loved him dearly. I still remember the first day I had him. He sat on my lap and I thought how wonderful he was as I stroked him. He looked up at me and I looked back – it was a love that lasted all his life. He was with me when I made the transition from single girl to married woman and then to mother. I loved him dearly and when he died I couldn't think of replacing him with another Golden Retriever. The vet visited us at home so that he could be put to sleep peacefully there with me at his side, gently stroking him.

Crispin had a huge influence on my future dog-training work. He was my introduction to competitive obedience and dog shows and to the thrill of working successfully with a responsive dog. I taught him to do all sorts of things, from carefully carrying an egg in his mouth without breaking it, to helping me weed the garden. I trained him on my own and learned just how much fun that could be for both of us, rather than using the formal methods of dog-training clubs. I used to swim with Crispin who would pull me along in the water and also taught him to fly a kite which was something a bit different.

Colleen

1970–85. My nanny dog and another Golden Retriever with a rich, glossy golden coat. She was a wedding present from the director of Buxted Chicken Company and his wife, and was intended as a companion for Crispin. She guarded our sons in their pram and happily played with them. She also went on to have two litters of her own, giving me the perfect opportunity to watch the behaviour of a mother dog and her puppies as they grew up and developed individual traits. Colleen was very much Fred's dog. It was to him that she went when we first viewed her as a tiny puppy, pulling on his shoelaces, and her gentle, quiet nature always appealed to him. When I had a burst eardrum and went temporarily deaf, Colleen helped, warning me if a car was coming. Later, when she was old and deaf herself, the roles were reversed. This was one of the many times when I have found hand signals absolutely vital.

Cassie

1979–91. She was my first Newfoundland and a real water baby. She arrived with us at eight weeks old, a fluffy, matt-black bundle of fur, looking more like a bear cub than a puppy. Our eldest son was just nine years old then and the youngest still a baby. At the time I also kept lots of chickens that she helped me with. She would carry their food, water and eggs for me. When she heard their startled cackling she would patrol the field and frighten off any inquisitive foxes. The chickens knew her well and were instantly quiet and content again. She also protected me from one or two aggressive cockerels I had at the time. Cassie was an excellent swimmer, always ready to plunge into any available water. We did lots of water work together and she successfully competed in the Newfoundland Water

Trials and obedience competitions. My best memories are of the regular snowy winters when Cassie pulled a sledge with David on it, running alongside Barry and Michael. Dogs were allowed into school playgrounds in those days and Cassie helped teach children in two playschools their road drill, among other things. The children loved seeing her and still remembered her when they were grown up. Carrying on my family tradition, Cassie met David from the village primary school at the end of the day and carried his lunch box to the car. Rather more unusually, I taught her to lead Eliza on a long expanding lead along the lanes. As well as being a wonderful family dog, she was also a lovely show dog and performed well at championship shows, gaining a challenge certificate. She was qualified for Crufts and it was wonderful showing her there.

Eliza
1985–2003. She was a long-haired red Miniature Dachshund and my courageous tracker. I'd never forgotten Susie, the Miniature Dachshund belonging to the family I worked for in Sweden, and Eliza was bought as a result of that. She would happily gallop along on walks and was intrepid when following a scent or leading us safely home after I'd got us lost, but in the evening she would curl up in a ball on the sofa for a cuddle with me. She was with me for eighteen years and I still miss her. She was a wonderful, happy, clever little dog who adored her games. Even as an old dog, she loved our special times together, playing or just sitting quietly.

When she was middle-aged, she became paralysed and went through quite a dangerous operation. It was her incredible courage recovering from that operation, several strokes and disabilities, which taught me so much about the importance of nursing, encouragement and love. When

I collected her from the veterinary college hospital in Cambridge, an elderly lady told me that the Queen had watched Eliza swim. I assumed she must be confused but apparently it was true. The Queen had visited the hospital. She went along to see the new hydrotherapy pool where Eliza was exercising as part of her treatment and had indeed seen her swim.

Christie

1992–2003. My second black Newfoundland. She was such a big, strong dog, rather high-spirited and naughty as a youngster, especially testing when an adolescent. Michael was at home a great deal when she was a puppy and they formed a specially close bond. He loved her strength and exuberance. He went away to Africa to teach for a couple of years, and when he returned Christie was overjoyed to see him again, and Michael was equally thrilled that she hadn't forgotten him after so long a time. It was with Christie that I began much of the work that Connie now does. She was my first assistance dog and home help because during the years she was with me my hips deteriorated to such a degree that eventually I needed both replaced. It was my success in training Christie and benefiting from the help she had given me that made me confident enough to attempt to teach Connie while I had such severe health problems.

Connie

2005. This book says it all. Thank you!

Dog Training Guide

Simple advice on
behavioural problems

Some Helpful Ground Rules

- Remember to start teaching a puppy at nursery not degree level, and begin the training from day one when you first bring your puppy home.
- Once you have established the house rules, be consistent and stick to them.
- Reward good behaviour and ignore unwanted behaviour whenever possible.
- Prevention is always better than cure – don't let bad habits start.
- Let sleeping pups lie.
- Begin short gentle grooming sessions while your puppy is still young so that it is relaxed and confident when groomed and handled as an adult.
- Five, five-minute training sessions rather than one, twenty-five minute lesson will help your dog learn faster.
- Teach hand signals alongside verbal commands for work and play. This means you can always communicate with your dog, and is especially useful if a dog loses hearing or becomes deaf in old age.
- To encourage a quick response from your dog, for instance coming when you call, use a high, excited voice and rapid hand and body signals.
- When you want your dog to be quiet and still, for example a down stay, use a low, calm voice and keep all your hand and body movements slow.

- A new pet arriving? Plan well in advance and carefully supervise gradual introductions to the resident pets.
- Bored and frustrated dogs make their own amusements with teeth, paws and claws.
- Walks, work and play keep a dog happy every day!

My Basic Guide to Problem Solving Strategies

As I have already said, the basic principle of problem solving is to reward the good and eliminate the unwanted behaviour.

- First find the reason for the problem behaviour.
- Remember, dogs *do not learn* if they are fearful, in pain, stressed, very excited or bored. They *do learn* if they are interested and rewarded.
- Dogs are generally motivated by one or more of: Food, Fuss, Freedom and Fun.

When a problem has arisen:
- Desensitise – through very gradual exposure to the problem.
- Distract – divert the dog's attention from what he is doing or thinking about doing.
- Extinguish – when a dog has learned a particular pattern of behaviour or bad habit, it will be extinguished if it is not reinforced by attention or reward.
- Time Out – this simply means you leave the room for a few minutes (not hours!) when your dog misbehaves. You should then return and carry on as normal.
- Ignore – when it is not practical to use the Time Out method, simply ignoring the dog can work well.

171

Try to remember that dogs are not 'being bad', 'teaching us a lesson' or 'taking their revenge' through problems such as messing in the house or chewing your possessions, neither are they 'expressing guilt'. It is our attitude and disapproving actions and body language which prompts the guilty-looking response. The dog really doesn't know that he has been bad but is simply worried and fearful when confronted by his cross owner.

After ripping his owner's clothing and wetting on them (which is a typical reaction of a dog suffering from stress and anxiety) the dog will probably curl up and go to sleep. If the owner returns at that point the dog will think he is being punished for sleeping which exacerbates the problem, causing more stress and anxiety.

Puppy Training

Ten Simple Steps for Trouble-free Toilet Training

It's worth remembering at the outset that young puppies, just like babies, cannot control their bodily functions so they should never be punished if they have an accident indoors. Again, like human babies, training times vary. Some puppies are toilet trained by eight weeks, others can take as long as a year to be fully reliable.

1 Indoors, place newspaper or puppy training paper over a large area around your puppy's bed. Ideally this should be on an impervious surface which is easily cleaned. The kitchen is often the ideal room as it is usually warm and much used, which ensures the new puppy has plenty of company, but do position his bed and paper in a quiet corner so that he has a retreat.

2 Look out for special puppy mats which can be used for toilet training instead of newspaper. They are made of absorbent paper and have a waterproof, non-slip backing which protects the floor and won't break down when wet. Most are permeated with a scent to encourage the puppy to use it.

3 Gradually reduce the area of paper once your puppy has established his favourite toilet area.

4 Outside, it is most important to go out to the garden

with your puppy and stay with him while you are training him to use the garden as his toilet.

5 Always take your puppy outside when he wakes, after meals and at intervals throughout the day. While he is performing keep repeating 'Be busy' (or whatever special word you want to use) in a happy voice. Your puppy will soon learn what this word means and will perform on command which is invaluable. Always praise enthusiastically!

6 Some puppies are reluctant to perform in the garden. To overcome this, gradually place the paper closer to the door until eventually you can move it outside. It helps to use a piece of soiled paper at this stage.

7 While unsupervised, the puppy should be confined to his familiar room with the paper on the floor. Remember, puppies are very likely to perform in a strange room in the house, especially on a new carpet. This can still happen, and frequently does, even when the puppy is apparently toilet trained.

8 To avoid accidents, when first taking your puppy into a different room, keep him on a lead or on your lap – puppies often sneak behind the sofa to perform so keep an eye on him and don't forget to take him to his toilet area at frequent intervals so he doesn't succumb to the excitement of a new room.

9 Other factors which can trigger accidents include fear, excitement and anxiety.

10 It generally helps to watch your puppy carefully so you recognise the early warning signs telling you he needs to perform. Also remember, if he makes a mistake, it is probably not his fault.

Lead Training

The first step is to get your puppy used to wearing a soft collar. Start as soon as your puppy arrives. To begin with, try putting on the collar just before a meal as this will help distract him.

Once he seems happy with the collar you can move on to the next stage and attach a lead. Show him a toy at the same time and let him play as you walk along. This will keep your puppy's attention on the toy which will distract him from biting the lead. These early lessons can start indoors and progress to the garden.

Ask another family member to walk ahead and call the puppy. Keep the lead loose while he follows them, walking alongside.

Just before dinner, carry your puppy to the far end of the garden and then let him lead you back to the house – and his meal. When he is old enough to go outside the garden, use the same method. Carry him a little way along the road and let him walk home on the lead. This method is so much kinder (and more effective) than dragging the frightened puppy away from his familiar home.

You can also teach your puppy to walk beside you off the lead. Encourage him to stay close to you by keeping his interest on a toy. After a few successful steps you should reward him by having a game with the toy. You can also use a tasty treat instead of a toy.

If lead training is carried out carefully and sensitively it will avoid common problems such as: the puppy sitting or lying down and simply refusing to move; wrapping a paw around the lead making it impossible to walk; rolling over and over so the walk cannot continue; attacking the owner's feet and legs – very painful; biting the lead; gripping the lead and dragging the hapless owner along behind – not so funny when the puppy is a Newfoundland or Mastiff and stronger than his owner!

Puppies Chewing

All puppies need to chew for their teeth to develop properly. They also use their mouths to investigate new objects, rather like young babies who automatically put things into their mouths. Chewing and sucking are generally comforting and help reduce stress. Anything with a lot of their owner's scent such as underwear or spectacle arms are particularly inviting. Chewing is natural for puppies and can't be avoided, but it is important to direct any chewing onto suitable objects, away from our valued possessions.

The cardinal rule is to be watchful to prevent unwanted chewing. Once a puppy has decided he likes the taste of wallpaper, it is very hard to encourage him to change his mind. This is one bad habit you don't want to allow to start.

Useful Distractions

Provide your puppy with a wide variety of safe, chewable objects – just like children, they quickly tire of their familiar toys and want something new and exciting.

Puppy Toy Boxes

Try making up several toy boxes and give him just one at a time so you can swap them around. Include cardboard boxes of all sizes – cereal packets and large boxes – you can hide secret edible goodies between the cardboard layers. An old terry nappy or towel tied through a hole in one end of the box is popular because it can be pulled around the room. Kitchen paper rolls can also be fun. An old shoe or slipper could be added but buy them from a charity shop so they smell quite different from yours – you don't want your puppy to think he can chew on your shoes! Many other goodies are readily available in pet shops including bones, special safe rubber toys, chews and rope toys which are designed to be good for developing teeth. The more varied you can make the boxes the better. As your puppy gets older and understands more, you can hide a new box for him to find to add to his fun.

Again just like small children, puppies need to be taught to play and learn when you play with them. Young puppies are not capable of amusing themselves without getting into mischief. Encourage him to investigate and bite his cardboard box by making exciting scratching noises on it – you could even bite on it yourself if you fancy it! Roll his toys, hide them and help him to find them. Teach him the command 'chew chew' so that he learns what he is allowed to bite. It's obviously just as important to teach 'no bite' and 'gently gently', said in a firm, quiet voice.

If your puppy does pick up one of your shoes, do not get cross but encourage him to bring it to you, telling him how clever he is and immediately offering him an especially inviting toy or tasty titbit. Avoid trying to pull the shoe from his mouth as his natural instinct will simply be to grip even harder. Instead, hold the shoe gently while you tempt him with his reward. Chasing after the puppy is also a big mistake as he will just think it's all part of the game. It may seem odd, but try running away from him to encourage him to come to you, this works well especially if you are playing with one of his toys as you go.

When your puppy is about to chew, or is already chewing something forbidden, immediately say, 'No chew' firmly, and distract him with one of his own toys. It is fine to warn a puppy while he is still only thinking about doing something but it will not work to reprimand him afterwards as he will simply not understand what he has done wrong.

Play Biting

Why Puppies Bite

Play biting is a natural part of puppy development and socialisation and a necessary part of the learning process. When a puppy bites its littermate too hard the hurt pup yelps and immediately stops playing. In this way puppies learn to use their teeth gently. Puppies also play with and bite their mothers. They lick and nip at her mouth for food. This is a very strong natural instinct – mother wolves, and even other members of the pack, will regurgitate food for the young cubs and many domestic bitches still do this. Lunging open-mouthed at their mother's face is a sign of affection. Puppies love to hang onto their mother's ears and pounce on and worry her thick furry tail. When the puppy gets too rough its mother reprimands it with a quick growl or gentle bite. Her other tactic is to remove herself from the puppy, either by jumping onto a convenient high place or by simply running away, remaining away from the puppy until it behaves, when she happily resumes play.

Unlike dogs and wolves, we humans are not covered in thick fur. Our bare hands, ankles and especially faces are extremely vulnerable to needle sharp teeth. Puppies find it confusing and cannot understand why we don't want to play their biting games. It's up to us to teach the puppy in a kind and tactful way that it must not use its teeth on us. Games with a puppy should be gentle and he should be encouraged to only bite his own toys and chews.

Helpful habits

- Always keep toys or chews handy so your puppy can be quickly distracted, ideally before he tries to bite your fingers. If he is over-excited and does inflict a painful nip, emulate the littermate and give a loud shriek, so he knows he has hurt you.

- Another method, if the puppy is lunging and biting, is to turn away so he has no eye contact – fold your arms and keep still and quiet. Often the puppy, puzzled by your behaviour, will sit and think about it for a second. As soon as he does this, immediately turn back to him, quietly praising and making a fuss of him, at the same time offering a suitable object to test his teeth on.

- If the situation escalates do not get cross but immediately remove yourself from the room, just as the natural parent would. This need only be for a few minutes. The puppy may also get over-excited in the garden during play and start biting. When this happens, immediately turn your back and stand quite still and quiet. When he has calmed down continue playing with him, being careful not to over-excite him again. I've found this method very effective.

- Your puppy's affectionate loving gesture of an open-mouthed lunge at your face is not really a bite and is not meant to hurt. However, this can be a problem as a sharp tooth can scratch your face, catch your eye and even go right through your lip! The best way of dealing with this is to teach the puppy to sit when being fussed over and also teach the word 'Lick' or 'Kiss'. He will very quickly learn to be gentle. Another method is to encourage him to come and greet you with a present in his mouth.

179

Puppy Grooming

Problems encountered at grooming time commonly include puppies fighting their owner while struggling to escape, biting and growling at their owner, biting and growling at the brush and running off with the brush. The puppy may also refuse to have his ears, paws, nails and teeth handled or looked at.

Avoiding problems

It is vitally important to establish an enjoyable grooming routine when you first have your puppy. Grooming and regular inspection helps to establish a sound base for a good relationship where the puppy learns to accept handling in a confident and enjoyable way. This early training makes life so much easier later when dealing with awkward grooming tangles or in giving eardrops, and smoothes the way for hassle-free examinations at the vet's. Another important reason for frequently handling your puppy at home is that any lumps or other medical conditions are quickly spotted and can be treated early.

Method One

Groom quietly and gently while the puppy is asleep. Groom whatever part is accessible and leave the rest until another time. Do not hurt him or make him jump by pulling at a tangle. This is a peaceful way of grooming which probably reminds the puppy of his mother's grooming.

Method Two

This method is useful when your puppy is in a lively, playful mood. Put aside a special toy, bone or chew which is only brought out at grooming time. This should be produced with great excitement to keep the puppy's interest. Tie this object to your foot, ankle or a handy chair, otherwise your puppy may run away with it. It is not always practical to hold the toy and brush at the same time. He must be encouraged to play with his special prize to divert his attention away from the brush which he will find enticing. It is impossible to groom a puppy while he is attacking the brush or your hand and this is a very bad habit that should not be allowed to start.

Method Three

As a separate exercise teach the commands 'Sit', 'Down' and 'Stand'. 'Roll over' is also very useful – it will allow you to brush his tummy easily, check for tangles under his armpits and for knots between his pads.

Tell the puppy to sit, then show him a titbit so he is focused on it while you gently brush his chest and ears. Feed him tiny pieces of the treat as you groom. Your voice should be quiet and calm as you tell him what a lucky puppy he is. A high, excited voice or quick movements with the brush will immediately turn your angelic puppy into a struggling, biting fiend! Gradually reduce the titbits until you just give one for good behaviour at the end of the session. It is also important in the early stages to keep grooming sessions short and successful. Do not be tempted to carry on until the puppy is bored and has started behaving badly.

Practise grooming in different areas and when you check his ears, teeth and paws, say the word so he gets to know where he is going to be examined. It is also a good idea to let other people gently handle the puppy so he is relaxed and confident around people generally. Not only will it be less stressful at the vet's but if you intend to show your dog he will stand well for the judge's examination.

Method Four
If you are still having trouble grooming a difficult puppy try moving him into a different room or the garden where he has something interesting to watch. Bad behaviour is often associated in the puppy's mind with a particular place. This crafty tactic works very well for all kinds of problems.

Enjoying Your Dog

To fully enjoy life with your dog it's important to know how to train or work with him. This really is not being harsh or onerous, it's simply understanding what your dog is fully capable of and helping him to live a fulfilled life. It's very easy to underestimate dogs and many of the problems I've come across as a behaviourist are simply because intelligent, naturally active breeds are bored and underutilised. Happy dogs work, rest and play!

The Benefits of Work and Training

- Builds up understanding and the bond between pet and owner.
- The dog becomes more intelligent – this has been proved!
- You gain pride in your dog and good public relations.
- It's fun for dog and owner.
- Dogs love the extra attention.
- It stops unwanted behaviour.
- It relieves frustration and boredom.
- It is specifically beneficial for young dogs.
- Keeps owners and dogs physically and mentally fit.
- As my experiences show, it really is useful.

Suit the Job to the Dog

Hounds for scent work, Gun dogs to fetch and carry, Newfoundlands for water work. Research your own breed and discover what it was originally used for. This is a chance to channel your dog's natural instincts.

Ask yourself how your dog can help you, utilising:

- Nose: for scent work, for example, finding lost car keys, gloves dropped on walks, tracking, 'finding' games.
- Mouth: fetching, carrying, holding, picking up dropped objects, taking messages, barking on command.
- Hearing: giving warning when something is wrong, hearing the door bell, phone, crying babies, lost animals for example crying kittens shut in a cupboard, even an intruder.
- Paws: particularly in toy breeds which enjoy shaking hands, waving bye bye, miming 'I'm shy' by hiding eyes behind paws. Gentle and often vital communication, particularly when working for the deaf.
- Strength: pulling carts, helping their owner out of chairs, up steep slopes and safely down slippery slopes.
- Therapy: patting dogs has been scientifically proven to lower blood pressure. Benefits to the elderly include people possibly living longer and healthier lives with fewer heart attacks than people who don't keep pets.
- Benefits to children: teaches responsibility. Reports suggest that children who are brought up with dogs may benefit from this in their forming of human relationships, they also tend to have fewer allergies.
- Professional dogs: guide dogs, dogs for the deaf and disabled, mountain rescue, drug detection – even a miniature Dachshund has been used successfully for this work. If the professionals can teach dogs all these

different tasks, you can certainly teach your dog to be useful in your everyday life.

- Outside help: it may be that you find training with other owners and dogs helpful. Look at what clubs are available in your area for puppies, and also obedience and ring-craft classes. You may also want to consider entering dog shows. There are championship, open, companion, agility, working trials and many more specialist activities to choose from.

Games and Play

The Benefits of Play

Play provides enjoyment for people and dogs. If taught to play as a puppy, your dog will still be having fun when he is old. Playing games cements a bond between a dog and his owner and helps teach him to watch for verbal and hand signals. Dogs become very clever at reading their owners' body language so they appear to know exactly what is wanted without being told. Games heighten and improve intelligence and the more a dog learns the more it is capable of learning: like stretching a piece of elastic, the more you stretch the longer it gets. Games provide an outlet for energy especially during bad weather when you may not be walking so far, and they help prevent a build-up of tensions and frustrations which often affect puppies and young dogs, which in turn can lead to behaviour problems.

Play has an important role in preventing and curing a wide range of behavioural problems such as destructiveness, chewing, boredom, biting hands and ripping at clothes. Aggression towards other dogs and people can be greatly overcome through play. Dogs such as Collies, which love to chase joggers and bicycles, can often be cured by substituting a game of chase-the-ball instead.

It doesn't matter what age you are, you can still enjoy

playing with your dog. Many games can still be enjoyed while sitting in a chair, at a table or just using one room. You can obviously also use the whole house, in the garden, walks and even the car – where games can be invaluable in teaching a young puppy not to be fearful.

Learning Through Play

Professionals have realised for some time the value of games and play in teaching dogs the most serious of jobs, including drug detection and finding explosives, and because the dogs enjoy the process so much they are very keen to work.

Games can and should be used to teach all the basic obedience exercises and simple scent work. It is so much easier to teach 'Sit', 'Down', 'Stand' and walking to heel using a toy rather than old methods which required pulling and pushing the dog into various positions which they naturally resist. By having fun, your dog will learn all these exercises without fear, and because they are so enjoyable, these early lessons will be stamped indelibly on his mind for life. Using these gentle, fun games to teach means that training can begin when a puppy is just a few weeks old as long as the play sessions are kept very short. You will find that older dogs will also respond well to your new-style lessons.

Becoming Pack Leader

Incorporating exercises such as 'Leave', 'Stay', and 'Give' into games subtly teaches your dog his position in the human pack. As the owner and pack leader, you should keep your dog's toys and only bring them out for these special games and it is also up to you to decide when to end the games and put the toys away. This indicates very clearly that you are the pack leader. Lots of people make the mistake of just leaving the toys out, expecting their dog or puppy to think up games and amuse himself. I am often called in to see how the dog then occupies himself, happily chewing the table leg while the toys are ignored.

Games to Avoid

- Do not play rough games especially with a large, powerful dog. This teaches the dog that he is bigger and stronger than his owner and that he is leader of the pack. It also teaches him to grip things and not give them up.
- Jumping at or on people in games should also be avoided. They may seem fine with you, but could be a disaster for a young child or an elderly visitor. Your dog simply will not understand why this 'game' is fine at some times and not at others.
- Even something simple like shaking hands must be taught carefully as it can lead to accidents. If a big dog has been taught to offer a paw to everyone, he could easily scratch a child's face which would be at just the right height.
- Over-exciting a dog can also be dangerous. Years ago, my youngest son was playing ball in the garden with my young, very heavy Newfoundland. They were both enjoying a boisterous game of chase with my son running away with the ball. Our Newfoundland charged into him knocking him to the ground where he hit his head. Luckily he was not badly hurt but even gentle dogs do not remember their own strength when excited.

When teaching new games, always remember to teach the 'Off' switch at the same time. My grandmother proudly taught her Spaniel to 'ask', i.e. bark, for a titbit. The only problem was that she failed to teach him to stop, so mealtimes were accompanied by the constant barking of a very vocal Spaniel. Also beware the bullying dog that will nag his owner for attention or not accept that the game is over. Have a clear signal that a game is finished and stick to it, not forgetting to reward your dog when the session is over.

Choosing Toys

Different breeds like different kinds of games and toys. Gun dogs usually love to retrieve and carry things, Terriers like pretend prey animals such as squeaky toys because they were originally bred to catch and kill rats. My Dachshund loved me to hide a toy under a rug so that she could find it by scent then burrow under the rug to find it, just as her ancestors would have done when they were burrowing for rabbits. Sheepdogs have very strong instincts to chase anything that moves so it is a good idea to give them substitute sheep to chase such as balls. If this chasing instinct is not channelled into something that is exciting and harmless, the Sheepdog will find his own 'work' to do, often with disastrous results, or he may develop serious behaviour problems.

Keep a selection of different toys – 'killing' toys like squeakies, 'running away' toys such as balls, throwing toys such as Frisbees, cone shaped rubber toys which bounce unpredictably are particularly popular with Lurchers, balls on a short length of rope which can be thrown a long way, and 'hedgehogs' with short plastic spikes all over which make them safer than a shiny wet ball. Warning: if you have both a large and small dog, make sure that the big dog cannot swallow the little one's toys!

The next group of toys are the chewing toys such as hide chews. Rubber, nylon or hard plastic bones are clean alternatives which will not make a mess on carpets. Puppies love shredding cardboard boxes, including cereal packets and the cardboard tube inside kitchen or wrapping paper. Another useful group of toys to keep are the 'comfort' type such as sheepskin teddies. The larger pet stores keep a wonderful selection of all these groups of toys.

If you have a problem with your dog chewing up all his toys teach him what he can safely chew on and really encourage him to bite these toys – use the word 'chew chew' so he understands he is allowed to bite. With other toys and your own possessions which you want him to carry without biting, teach the word 'gently', then if he is too rough take the toy away for a short time before trying again, praising him for being careful. I have successfully taught dogs to carry eggs without breaking them and to fetch my watch for me.

For times when you are too busy to play, make up two or more play boxes filled with indestructible and chewing toys. Only give your dog one box at a time so you always have a new and exciting selection of toys in reserve. Like young children, the new, interesting toys will hold your dog's attention far longer.

Games to Play

Build up all games gradually, one step at a time. Start by making them very simple, help your dog and show him what you want so that it is easy for him to be successful. As the dog becomes more proficient, you can gradually make the games harder. Always reward him with praise, making the game exciting but not so much that things get out of control – young children playing with dogs should always be supervised. Only repeat the game about three times or your dog will become bored. Remember that older dogs which have never been taught to play will need extra motivation to get them started.

- Hide the toy – behind furniture, in another room or the garden. Either ask someone to hold the dog or shut him in another room while you do the hiding.
- Choose a toy – line up the toys on the floor and either hold your dog or ask him to sit and stay while you arrange the toys. Then let him choose his favourite. My Dachshund loved this game and would sit and watch with great excitement as I set out her toys, particularly when I squeaked each toy as I put it down.
- Find the titbit – hide it somewhere in the room, or underneath one of a line of objects such as plastic flowerpots and let your dog sniff along the line to find it.
- Find the person – one person hides in another room, the garden or on a walk, and the dog has to find them by scent. Make this very easy at first.
- Find the toy, glove, etc – outside when it is hidden under leaves, in undergrowth or under snow.
- Swap the toy – you play this sitting down. Throw one toy and encourage your dog to bring it back to you. Have another toy in your pocket or on your lap (squeaky toys are good for this) and as he brings you the first toy, squeak the second one, show him how exciting it is and say 'Give', taking the first toy and immediately throwing the second one. A variation on this is to sit with your dog and show him a toy. Wriggle it around to make it seem interesting and when he goes to grab it say, 'Hold'. After a moment say, 'Give', while showing him a titbit. If you feed him a small piece, he will immediately release his toy. Most dogs will happily relinquish a toy for a tasty treat. Very gradually build up the time he holds the toy. Again, only repeat this two or three times, so your dog doesn't get bored. Swapping one toy for another is invaluable in teaching a dog to give up any possession – never try to pull

anything from his mouth as this will automatically make him grip harder.

- Catch the ball or toy – encourage your dog to walk backwards by walking towards him pretending to throw the ball. Then say 'Sit', 'Stay', before actually throwing the ball shouting 'Catch'. You can then have a game of chase. Because I have always wanted my Newfoundlands to pull a cart or sledge, I find the game brilliant for teaching them to walk backwards.

- Leave the titbit – teach your dog the 'Down' command. Place a titbit on one paw, say 'Leave' and watch him carefully. If you think he is about to cheat, put your hand over the treat. When you start only leave it there for a second before saying 'OK', or 'Eat'. The length of time can be gradually built up until he has several treats on each paw. My Newfoundland goes on lying there hoping for more – she doesn't want the game to finish as she is so greedy!

- Teach the names of different toys. Start by throwing one toy and saying 'Fetch the ball', then put out another toy and run towards it with your dog, saying 'Fetch the squeaky', continue adding toys but only when your dog has thoroughly learnt the name of each one.

Fun Training Games

- Remember to always use a special word to mark the end of an exercise, such as 'OK' or 'Finished' which should be said in an excited voice.

- 'Sit' – when the dog is standing show him a toy, wriggle it about to gain his interest, then move it back above his head. To see it he will naturally sit and as he does, say 'Sit' then praise him and play.

- 'Down' – have your dog in the sit position, hold a titbit

in your hand in front of his nose, then gradually lower it to the floor in a diagonal line so that he has to reach forward to get it. Most dogs will lie down to reach it. Say the word 'Down' as he does this, then praise. Down can also be taught by getting a toy to 'run away' under a low stool. As the dog tries to reach it he will have to lie down.

- 'Down, Stay' – teach as the above but have something your dog can nibble in your hand while he is in the down position and say the word 'Stay'. For both the Down and Stay exercise, use a low long drawn out tone.
- Heel work – this should be done off the lead. The game teaches the dog to keep close to your left side, and it needs to be fun. Let him see you have an exciting squeaky toy in your hand and hold it so he has to keep close to you to get near it. Sometimes let the toy 'hide' in your pocket, then bring it out again, giving the odd squeak. Only walk a few paces at first then throw the toy and have a game, gradually increasing the distance he walks to heel, changing direction and pace from fast to slow.
- Another simple way to teach your dog what you want is simply to wait until he does it naturally and then say the appropriate word. Lots of things can be taught like this including rolling over, shaking hands, waving goodbye. I recently met a delightful little dog who would hide her eyes with her paws when her owner asked, 'Are you shy?' Dogs love the attention and admiration they receive when they can demonstrate how clever they are.

Jumping Up

It helps to remember that it is natural for dogs to jump up. In the wild a cub licks its mother's lips to persuade her to regurgitate food and it will beg food from other adults in the pack. Our domestic bitches still have this instinct and will sometimes vomit up an extra dinner for her puppies. Leaping up, nipping and licking at other dogs' muzzles is all part of canine socialising. Because jumping up is so instinctive we have to substitute another activity which is both enjoyable and acceptable for the dog, its human family and their visitors.

- Prevention is always much easier than cure, so ideally a puppy should never learn to jump up.
- Always get down to your dog's level and make a fuss of him while he has all four paws on the ground.
- When playing games or giving a reward, always remember to hold the object low so that the dog never forms the habit of jumping to reach what he wants.
- Excitement causes a young dog to jump up, so do not greet him with too much enthusiasm. The problem with visitors arriving is that we often greet them in high-pitched excited voices and they greet the dog and us in the same way. Dogs are great mimics and copy our behaviour – so we should keep calm.

Prevention and Cure

To stop a dog from jumping up try the following:

- Practise control exercises, sit and down stays.
- Teach 'Go to bed' for a special treat.
- Teach 'Sit' for a titbit, then when visitors arrive, let them give the titbit, but insist on the 'sit'.
- Train your dog to bring a present to you when you greet him and encourage him to take this present to any visitors. A heavy dog blanket or bed that dangles over his legs works well as it is difficult to jump up with it. Tell your dog how clever he is so that he enjoys this exercise. Gun dog breeds love to carry gifts.
- Lively dogs such as Terriers which find it difficult to keep still can be trained to chase a special 'prey' toy that rolls, squeaks or bounces in an erratic way or a woolly rat which can be 'killed' when visitors arrive. Practise so that the dog is hooked on this toy and then keep it for visitors to give to him. Remember to remind them to keep their hands low down when they give it to him.
- You can also try shutting the dog away while you settle your guests. When all is calm and quiet, you can introduce the dog. If he is allowed to smell their coats etc. before coming in, he is more likely to be controllable.
- Dog mealtimes are an excellent time for visitors to arrive. Mix up your dog's dinner just before they appear, then when they come in, feed him. He will be far more interested in eating than jumping up.

Always pick a method which suits the breed and temperament of your particular dog.

Jumping up when out walking is a common problem. When dogs reach adolescence they become very curious and like to investigate and socialise with any new people they meet. This is a natural part of their development. When they are older, they become more discriminating and not so interested in strangers but while they are going through this early stage, try to prevent them from jumping up.

- When your dog is running loose, distract him with a toy or treat to keep his attention on you.
- Run away from your dog and encourage him to follow you.
- If your dog does rush up to someone, warn them to ignore him.
- If your dog is on a lead, teach him to sit and let other walkers offer him one of your biscuits.

Pulling on the Lead

One of the most common complaints I hear from dog owners is that their dogs pull on the lead. There are often a few simple reasons why they do this.

Think about where you are going. If you habitually walk your dog on a lead to the local park where he then has a free run and plays with other dogs, he is naturally going to find this prospect very exciting. He will pull on the lead to get there as quickly as possible, towing his owner along behind him. Here are two common scenarios.

The lamp post dog: this kind of dog can generally be seen dragging his owner along, often at the run, as he homes in on the next interesting lamp post. He then keeps his owner hanging around while he slowly investigates all the 'messages' that other dogs have left him. After leaving his own message he will set off at speed to the next enticing smell. Often the whole walk is dominated by the dog's behaviour, with the owner just tagging along at the other end of the lead.

The obsessive 'heel-work' owner: this person expects his dog to do close 'competition' heelwork thoughout the walk. The dog naturally finds this restrictive, tiring and boring. After a while he will gradually pull ahead until he is pulled back into the heel position. This pattern is repeated for the whole walk.

Prevention and Cure

- Ask yourself whether you actually need your dog to walk to heel. Use a longer lead and keep close heelwork for busy pavements and roads.

- Think about where you are walking. If you normally take your dog on the lead to the park, try a different route to get there. Try walking to another area for his free run, and think about circular routes which do not finish with a free run. This should stop him getting too excited at the start of the walk.

- Make heelwork fun. Practise heelwork 'games' on and off the lead, use treats and toys. Try squeaking a toy, or play with a ball as you walk along, keep the toy close to your side so your dog has to keep close to investigate. When he has walked just a few steps by your side throw the ball or toy and have a game, then repeat the exercise, encouraging him to keep by your side for a little longer each time.

- Using treats or toys to fix your dog's attention on you, play a game where he has to stay by your side as you keep changing pace and direction. Try running, skipping, or creeping very slowly along. When you go faster, encourage him with a high excited voice, when you go slowly whisper quietly to him. Don't forget to rustle that treat bag and reward him after each short session.

- In a quiet lane or verge, have your dog on a long lead. Start with your dog in the sit position, say 'Heel' and set off with a short, loose lead, keeping your dog's attention on you. If he walks just two or three paces with the lead loose, say 'Off you go', let out all the lead and actively encourage him to snuffle around in the hedges or grass. Repeat this exercise, gradually increasing the number of paces he walks to heel before he has his fun time. Dogs like Springer Spaniels respond very well to this technique.

- If you have a dominant dog that drags you from lamp post to lamp post and keeps you hanging around in the rain while he does his own thing, re-educate him. Be reasonable and find a mutual compromise. For example, insist that he walks nicely with you, not pulling, stopping or sniffing. Set off at a smart pace, don't let him slow up or stop, run so he has to keep up. Decide which places he can investigate. Do not let him stop in between the places you have decided on. Loosen the lead, encourage him to sniff around for a reasonable amount of time, then call him, setting off positively and smartly. It is most important not to give in to this kind of dog.
- When you go for a walk, remember and practise the 'heel-work' games, using treats, toys or both, changing the treats to keep him attentive. It is most important to make the walk on a lead fun and as interesting as a free walk.

If you have tried everything but your dog is still pulling on the lead, try:

- Abrupt left-hand turns, past the dog's nose.
- Left-hand circles.
- If the lead goes tight, he cannot progress. Stop or turn round and go back the other way. Do not give in, not even once.

Running off on walks

Another common problem which owners often bring to me is the dog that runs away on walks and refuses to come when called. It is natural for the dog to investigate scents, other dogs, animals and people. In the wild, a dog would not survive long unless it used its nose to track down food. It would also need to be alert and investigate new sights and signs which might be a threat to the pack. We humans must be a very poor substitute for a canine pack leader. We never help our dog catch a rabbit, we ignore all those exciting scents and don't bother to follow them. No wonder he abandons us on walks.

Some breeds naturally range at a distance while others have a very strong instinct to follow a scent, or pursue their quarry down holes.

Horses and other animals which run away can be irresistible and your dog's instinct to 'hunt the prey' will be very strong. Strangers, and particularly children with their quick movements and high voices, are especially inviting to a curious young dog. Joggers, for instance, may seem to a dog to be running away and thus provide an unwitting invitation to be chased. Dogs are social animals and enjoy meeting other dogs on their walks. They have strict rules of etiquette which must be followed before they can leave each other. If they like each other they often enjoy a game before joining their owners again.

Young puppies usually like to stay close to their owners where they feel safe but when they reach adolescence, they become bolder and want to explore further.

Prevention and Cure

- Make yourself far more exciting than all the other distractions on a walk.
- Take really tasty titbits along with you which you vary.
- Condition your dog at home to thoroughly enjoy his toys so that he responds happily to them when out on walks. Again, make sure you vary the toys to keep his interest.
- Include a squeaky toy to catch his attention: a 'prey animal' like a ball, or a furry animal on a piece of cord – these are easily made, maybe from a synthetic fur hat bought from a charity shop.
- Make the games exciting. Your dog will not respond or be motivated unless you are.
- Hide a toy in the undergrowth and encourage him to find it. When he does, have a game with him, don't just take the toy and walk on.
- Teach your dog to use his nose and track back along the path to find a dropped toy.
- Try to maintain the puppyhood stage where your dog is a little worried about losing you. Aim to have him looking to see where you are, what you are doing and which direction you are taking.
- Vary walks as much as possible. Try to take a different path without him noticing – obviously you need to keep an eye on him without him knowing in case he gets lost.
- Play hide and seek in undergrowth or behind trees and let him find you.

- Always try to make walks as fun and exciting as possible by changing your pace for instance. Try running away occasionally and let him catch you up.

Be vigilant when your dog is running free, and be on the lookout for people, sheep, horses or any other temptation. Young dogs love to rush up to strange people and if greeted enthusiastically, will often jump all over them. You must call your dog back quickly before he is too far ahead of you. Encourage him back with one of his special treats when he is running away and he will usually come. If you meet another dog, leave the two alone to make their introductions and do not hurry them. If possible give them time to play. When you want to continue, wait for a natural pause in the game and run away calling enthusiastically, dragging the fur toy behind you.

Another problem with adolescent dogs at the end of the walk is that they are reluctant to get back into the car and will therefore avoid capture. This situation usually cures itself as the dog gets older and enjoys car rides. Be aware of the problem and put your dog back on the lead well before reaching the car and play an exciting game with him. When you want him to get back into the car, give him a special treat and drink of water. An even better solution is to put the dog on his lead, begin to return to the car, then take a little extra walk. Always avoid the situation where you are getting really cross as you try to catch him, as he will remember the bad experience next time and be even more difficult to catch.

Handy hints

- Only call your dog back on a walk for pleasant things.
- Never call your dog to punish him.

205

- Avoid grabbing him, he will become hand shy and dodge out of the way.
- Do not shout or use any threatening gesture to get him to come.
- Make yourself inviting – crouching low, arms wide, encouraging voice – all these make it easier for a timid dog to approach.
- Only call your dog when you are certain he will come. It undermines your authority if he doesn't respond and he is more likely to ignore you next time.
- Practise recalls on a long, expanding lead where you have complete control.
- Occasionally call your dog back on a walk when there are no distractions, keep him at heel for a minute, feed him a treat and then release him again.
- Try timing your walk for just before mealtime. The dog is more likely to want to go home with you if he is hungry and dinner is waiting!
- Avoid, if possible, walking your dog at dawn and dusk when the scents of other animals are stronger and more exciting. These are also the times when rabbits come out which dogs find irresistible.
- In very difficult cases, the dog's dinner can be split into several portions and be fed to him on the walk. Every time the dog comes when called, you can feed him a portion of his dinner. If he does not come, he will miss a portion of food for that day. This should only ever be used on a healthy adult dog and as a last resort.
- If you have two dogs and they run away together, keep one on a lead and then swap over.
- Aim to have a dog that is always confident he will have a lovely welcome from you.

Garden Problems

Dogs That Will Not Come in From the Garden

This is a fairly common problem which can escalate to the point where it is impossible to encourage the dog indoors at all. I had one client whose dog spent the whole night in the garden because she could not get him inside. Another variation is the dog that comes to the door, barks to come in and when the door is opened runs back into the garden. A few moments later he returns, barks again and rushes away yet again.

Dogs that are wary of being caught or reluctant when called indoors usually have a very good reason for their behaviour. When I ask clients why they want their dogs to come inside, the answer is usually one or all of the following: 'Because I have to go to work/ go shopping/ do the school run . . . and need to shut him in.' The other reason is that the owner wants to go to bed. It is not surprising that the poor dog does not like coming indoors where he has unpleasant associations of being shut up and left alone.

The second problem, where the dog comes to the door and then runs away again, is his way of getting attention. He is bored and has probably found that these tactics entice his frustrated owner out to give chase all round the garden as he tries to catch him. These 'game' sessions help him relieve the boredom.

Prevention and Cure

- Do not call your dog in from the garden simply to shut him up when you go out, or when you go to bed.
- Plan your strategies. If you have to leave your dog at home, take him for a walk well before you go, bring him indoors on a lead and give him food, fuss and play, so that he enjoys being inside. It is important to do this early when your dog is still young, so he does not associate this attention with being left on his own.
- Only call your dog indoors for pleasant things. Make sure he is outside when it is time for food, walks, rides in the car and play.
- When your dog comes in from the garden offer him something tasty to eat.
- If you are going out without your dog, try to ensure he is indoors for about twenty minutes before you leave.
- Practise basic control in the house and garden, especially 'Come'. At first do this on a long lead and reward well.
- When your dog is loose in the garden, do not call him unless you are absolutely sure he will come. If he does not respond you may get extremely angry and frustrated which your dog will sense and this will have the effect of making him go as far away from you as possible, and make him very wary of coming indoors next time.
- At bedtime, take the dog out to relieve himself, on a lead at first, then give him another ten minutes alone before he is put to bed. It works well if you give him a biscuit and a drink of milk, or another favourite treat, as he is put to bed.
- A regular, enjoyable routine at bedtime that has no bad associations will soon have your dog happily running in from the garden.

The dog who keeps barking at the door and then runs away needs lots of play and games both indoors and in the garden. Dogs need people, they don't play on their own. It is no good putting your dog outside and expecting him to amuse himself. He will get horribly bored and will bark at the door, birds, neighbours, cars, dogs and people walking past his property. If he isn't doing that, he is quite likely to be digging holes in flowerbeds or making his escape by digging a hole under the fence to find excitement elsewhere. Let him help you in the garden by fetching and carrying, and find work for him indoors as well. Use your imagination, there are masses of different jobs dogs can do inside and outside the home.

Remember that if you are trying to get your dog to come to you or come indoors, never: chase, grab, lunge, shout, stare, lose your temper, have an aggressive body posture, throw things or hit him!

Escape from the Garden

Why does your dog want to escape from the garden or house? If you can understand the reason for the problem, it will help you find solutions.

- A dog that is frequently left on its own will quickly become bored and think life is more exciting outside the confines of the garden.
- A bitch in season anywhere in the neighbourhood can make a male dog very restless and desperate to get to her.
- Being pack animals, it is quite usual for two dogs to go off together to hunt.
- Sometimes the sole housedog will get out to call for its canine friend and they will go off hunting – it may be just rabbits, but could be something much more serious

like sheep worrying. One very sweet, loving housedog I know would get out and call for a Collie who lived nearby and they would go off to kill sheep.

- Some dogs want to find human or canine company if they are lonely or anxious.
- Sometimes they try to follow their owner to work and sadly people have been known to run over their own dog as it followed the car.
- Greedy dogs, or rescued dogs who have lived rough on the streets, often continue to try to get out to scavenge in dustbins, takeaway cartons or even to hoover up bird food from a neighbour's garden which is quite rewarding for them.

These are just a few of the reasons why the family dog decides to set off alone.

Preventing the problem

As always, prevention is better than cure. If a dog enjoys his outing and finds it rewarding, eating a tasty snack or enjoying the thrill of the chase perhaps, even just once or twice, he will continue to try to get out.

Start with physical restraints
- Check the fences and gates, not forgetting that dogs can get out of the smallest hole beneath a fence or through a hedge, or dig or chew their way out.
- A canine nose or paw can nudge a catch open on a gate. Remember they have plenty of time to work at it.
- Smooth surfaces are harder to climb, so if the fence or gate has horizontal supports fix a rigid panel of smooth wood or plastic to one side.
- Some very small dogs can jump great heights. A wire

mesh supported horizontally at the top of fences and gates on the garden side should prevent a dog jumping over. Interestingly when I had a Golden Retriever puppy I put up a flimsy very low fence to keep him in but as he had no desire to go off he never jumped it, even when he grew quite big.

- Electric fences could be used where it is impossible to confine a dog by any other means, such as on a large estate or farm. This should only be used when all other methods have failed and the only other solution is to rehome or have the dog destroyed.

- Some dogs start their bid for freedom from the house. I have known of bitches in season jumping from first floor windows to reach their suitors.

- Don't overlook cat flaps – I visited someone with a huge male German Shepherd and was amazed to see him easily go through the cat flap rather than wait for the door to be opened!

- Castration should help for the dog that is always going off to find a bitch in season. Although if he has been doing it for a long time he may enjoy the freedom to explore so much that he does not want to give it up even after castration.

Helpful Hints

- Play, work and companionship are the most important ways of keeping a dog happily at home. Even if you are busy, for example working in the garden, it is possible to keep your dog with you by having short play sessions at regular intervals. Try to involve him in work, fetching, carrying and finding things in the garden. Connie is too busy helping me to go off. She carries gardening tools, her bucket of pegs to the washing line and finds my lost gardening glove (she must wonder why I keep losing it) when I deliberately hide it for her to find. Dogs love working and being enthusiastically praised so much that they like to hang around waiting for more fun.

- If you have more than one dog and cannot keep an eye on all of them, it is amazing how fast they can vanish. The simple solution is to let only one out at a time.
- Food is very important. Always let your dog out before he is fed and call him in at meal times. If you have to leave your dog on his own in the garden for a while try some of these ideas. Use part of the daily ration as random treats scattered in the garden near the house; he should keep coming to check if you have put more there. Little and often works well, and it helps to add something really tasty. You could hide bones and other titbits in a compost heap or under a pile of leaves – again he will probably keep checking to see if there is something new. Hide tiny tasty-smelling titbits around the garden and make them hard to find so that he has to use his nose. Food cubes which he must push around with his nose or paw to get the food out should also help keep him occupied for some time.

My old Newfoundland Cassie was put out first thing in the morning for a rather long breakfast time to allow me to have a special one-to-one play with my little Dachshund, Eliza. The area was completely unfenced and the garden was surrounded by woods and fields. Rabbits, foxes and deer all came through the garden on their way to the woods but Cassie would not leave her special place on the steps by the back door, as she did not want to risk missing her random breakfast!

Barking Problems

Barking in the House

There are many reasons why dogs bark at home and to cure the problem you first need to work out why your dog is barking.

There are several main reasons to consider:

Attention seeking, dominance and excitement
This type of dog jumps up and down barking whenever he sees his lead, he barks for his dinner, or fetches a toy then barks until someone plays with him. He likes to be the centre of attention, especially when his tired owner is trying to relax or watch television.

Cure
Reward quiet, calm behaviour with praise and attention. Ignore the barking and never let your dog dominate you. If your dog barks when you pick up his lead, simply put it back down until he is quiet – you will probably find you have to repeat this several times at first. Another method is to teach him to hold his own lead or a toy – not many dogs can bark while holding something in their mouths and providing a dog with a positive task has a calming effect.

Barking for dinner can also be cured by giving the dog

something else to do – sit and stay is good, although you should make this exercise very short at first, so if your dog sits for a second without a sound, quickly feed him.

To stop a dog barking for games and attention, pack away all the toys and make sure it's always you who decides when to play and when to stop. Make it clear when games are over with a special command and with a treat that is given for a calm, quiet sit. Do not be bullied and give in if your dog insists on barking. Instead try one of the following:

- Make your dog leave the room, only for a minute, then let him in again *before* he barks.
- Alternately you can leave the room abruptly and return as soon as he is quiet.
- Another very successful method is to sit down, relax, pick up a large newspaper and read it, holding the paper in front of your face so your dog cannot make eye contact. Anybody else in the room should do the same. Keep this up until your dog is quiet, then immediately put the newspaper down so he can see your face, then very quietly praise him so he does not get excited again.

I successfully used this last method for a little Terrier that had barked, bullied and bitten his exhausted owners for nearly two years – he was cured in one and a half hours.

Guarding the house

This is the kind of dog that has decided it is his job to deter all potential burglars, including the postman and any visitors to the house. His work is made more enjoyable because he can usually rely on getting an instant excitable response from his owners. Barking at people walking past who always go away, and at the postman who comes up to the house, delivers something but doesn't dare come in, are also especially rewarding.

Cure
- Ignore all barking – this will be very difficult as it is self-rewarding for, although your dog is not now provoking a reaction from you, he will still be rewarded by the reactions of people outside the house.
- Another method is to give the dog something else to do instead of barking, such as fetching a ball or bringing you the post. I would insist on a silent sit by the door and supervise the post carrying, before rewarding with a titbit.

Barking at visitors can be cured in many ways:

- Keep a special 'visitor' toy – a large fluffy toy will make barking difficult when the dog has it in its mouth. Teach your dog to play with this well in advance of welcoming visitors.
- Some dogs respond well to a toy that they fetch or find.
- Food also works – try offering titbits in a crunchy bag or tin, which your dog should sit for quietly. Small pieces are particularly good, as the dog has to concentrate on that rather than barking.
- Never give a reward if the dog barks even slightly.
- Another method, if possible is to arrange to meet your visitors a little way from the house so the dog is not meeting them on his own territory. It is far less confrontational for you all to walk in the same direction as you enter the house, rather than the dog meeting visitors head on, maybe in the confines of a small hall. (Also see my notes on preventing dogs jumping up on pages 195–7.)

Frustration
Frustration is another common reason why a dog barks. The cat sitting on a high windowsill and staring at the dog, or birds hopping and fluttering about in their cage

215

where he cannot get at them, these situations are confusing for the dog, causing frustration.

Cure
In both these cases distraction works well. Often the dog has a particular time of day for these frustrations, so if you anticipate them, you can distract him with a chew, bone, or an interesting box of toys he can investigate.

Another very important cause of frustration is when your dog does not understand a command. Always make sure he knows exactly what you want.

Jealousy
In this situation the dog is quiet and relaxed all day until another member of the family returns home and then barking becomes one of his ways of gaining attention. Some dogs cannot stand their owner talking on the phone and will often bark or pull at their clothes to attract attention.

Cure
When a dog is jealous of a family member, he should be reassured that he is still loved and will have plenty of attention and games but only when he is quiet. Training your dog to greet the home-comer with a special present so he can be praised for bringing it and remaining quiet is also a good idea.

It's common for dogs to bark while their owner is talking on the phone, probably because they are confused and cannot understand what's happening.

- Keep a toy or chew by the phone ready to give to your dog when it rings. It is important to get the timing right so he is rewarded *before* he reacts to the phone, not afterwards.
- Another method would be to desensitise him by getting someone to keep ringing at a certain time to get him used to it.

216

- Many people rush excitedly to the phone and then have an animated conversation. Dogs always copy people, so if we are rushing around excitedly they will do the same! But if your phone is constantly ringing, and answered calmly, the dog would think it was very boring and probably go to sleep.

Insecurity and dependence

When a dog feels worried, anxious or insecure he will often bark or whine when left alone, especially at night when his owners have gone to bed. This can happen even with dogs that have previously been quite happy and relaxed.

This type of barking can have many different triggers:

- Moving house, especially if the dog is put to bed in a more isolated place in the house.
- Bereavement, if they are used to having the company of the other animal.
- A change of routine, or illness and pain can cause the dog to feel very dependent on his owner.
- As dogs age they can also become much more dependent, especially if their hearing and sight deteriorates. They can also become confused and disoriented. Stiff old joints can make it difficult for them to climb into their beds and get comfortable. Illness, drugs and old age can also cause toileting problems.

Cure

- Move the dog's bed as close to the main bedroom as possible, or into the bedroom if you are happy with that arrangement. If you do not want the dog in the room try leaving the bedroom door open with a baby gate across.
- Make sure your dog's bed is as warm and comfortable as possible.

217

- Try putting an old sweater, one you have just been sitting on or worn recently, in the dog's bed as you settle him for the night.
- A special comforting small meal at bedtime may also help.
- Make bedtime as quiet and relaxing as possible.
- Give your dog calm, soothing reassurance while he is still quiet during the night. Do not wait until the dog is barking and then try to quieten him as this will encourage him to bark for attention.
- If your dog has begun barking, wait for him to stop for a moment, then quietly talk to him.

Fear

Some dogs bark at people or objects that make them feel fearful or suspicious. Strange objects that the dog has not seen before, especially if they are black, can trigger this behaviour. Weird creatures that walk on their hind legs growling as they advance, for example, the new upright vacuum cleaner, can cause panic. Connie was terrified recently when I wheeled a large black suitcase into the house that she had not seen before.

Rescued dogs with unknown backgrounds, ones that have been badly treated, or dogs that have not been socialised can all have problems. Even people the dog is familiar with can upset him by suddenly appearing looking totally different. When I first had my Dachshund puppy, Eliza, I washed my hair and wrapped my head in a big towel – she did not recognise me and barked furiously. One rescued dog I went to see was terrified of men with big feet because one had kicked her. Another rescued dog I helped with was so terrified of one member of the family, who was very tall and wore glasses, that she hid behind the sofa barking hysterically whenever he was in the room.

Cure

Gradual, careful exposure to as many different objects as possible is the best approach. People who live in the house should practise walking about with a variety of things such as a walking stick, a large hat, a rucksack, or holding a baby or bulky bag.

- Do not surprise or frighten the dog, as this will make him worse. Talk to him as you approach and let him come up and sniff you as you reassure him.

If your dog is frightened of visitors, give him space and do not force him to meet them.

- Give him plenty of time to get used to strangers in his house.
- Ask your visitors to co-operate by completely ignoring the dog and not making any eye contact or movement towards him.
- If possible, arrange for your visitors to come inside, sit down and relax before the dog is invited in – the key being invited not forced!

Reward quiet behaviour with titbits or a game with his favourite toy. I visited one very worried little dog who settled and stopped barking very quickly, using this method. I asked her owner not to force her to come up to me. I sat down and ignored her while talking quietly to her owner, and lastly the daughter asked me if I would like to see all the things she had taught their dog. I was then entertained by a wonderful display of tricks and games that this little dog had learnt. This display was quite complex so needed the dog's full attention. Because she was praised so lavishly after each one she thoroughly enjoyed herself and most importantly she forgot all her fears.

Think carefully about situations where you will want your dog to bark, for instance if you really do have a burglar or there is a fire. Dogs have often saved lives by warning of danger and raising the alarm, say, if a baby or old person needs help. A dog has many different barks so it is important to learn what your dog is trying to tell you.

It can be useful to teach the commands 'Speak' and 'Enough' so your dog knows what you mean when you tell him to be quiet.

Dogs need to work, especially young ones, and if they are bored and frustrated in the home they will find work of their own which will probably not be to their owner's liking. Use your dog's natural working instincts. Teach your dog to fetch, carry, seek and find. I use my dog as an extra pair of hands to do all kinds of work indoors. Dogs love all the attention and praise they get when they work A relaxed, happy, occupied dog does not feel the need to relieve his frustrations in barking.

Barking in the Garden

Dogs that bark in the garden can cause more trouble between neighbours than almost anything else. These rows can lead to letters from councils and visits from dog wardens when irate neighbours eventually make official complaints.

There are many reasons why dogs bark in the garden but this problem can be prevented or cured when the reasons are understood and treated. In my experience, the main problem is the dog who is put out in the garden to amuse himself, often for long periods. He amuses himself, but not the neighbours!

Certain types of dog are more prone to barking than others. Terriers are high on the list, followed by active gun dogs such as Springer Spaniels and some of the guarding breeds. Young dogs are also more likely to rush around barking than a sleepy old dog who is content to doze in the sun. Puppies usually start off by being fairly quiet but quickly learn that they can get attention from their humans and achieve what they want by barking.

A dog has many different barks. If you can learn what each one means it will help you understand your dog and make it easier to treat the barking problem. For example, the 'greeting a friend' bark is very different from the deeper suspicious bark used to deter burglars. You can hear the difference when a dog thinks there is a stranger approaching. When he realises it is someone he knows, the bark changes to a happy welcome which is quite different. There is the short, quick, high-pitched 'invitation to play' bark which is similar to the frustrated one, except that the frustrated one is often kept up for some time. The lonely dog who is 'home alone' has a monotonous bark that he can keep up for hours. These are just a few examples and you will soon recognise others in your own dog.

Boredom
It is not surprising that the bored dog reacts by barking at anything he sees or hears if he is shut out and ignored with nothing but an ancient bone or an old discarded toy for company.

Cure
As far as possible keep your dog indoors unless you are also going into the garden. Make trips outside as interesting as possible, for example, teach your dog to carry your gardening gloves, hide behind the dustbin and let him find you, talk to him and practise simple commands such as sit, down, and come, and make it fun. If you really do need to put your dog outside on his own for a short time, plan ahead:

- Hide a new bone in the compost heap where he can enjoy digging for it without spoiling your flowerbeds.
- Hide small food treats all round the garden.

- Produce a new toy box full of really interesting items that he can chew and investigate.
- Give him a food ball or cube with food inside that he can chase round the garden.

Attention seeking

This dog thinks up all kinds of clever tactics to encourage his family outside to keep him company. A favourite one is to run up to the door and bark, as though he wants to come in, then as soon as someone appears he will run away hoping for a game. He then gives his owner time to sit down and pick up his newspaper before repeating the exercise. As he has nothing else to do he can keep this game up for hours.

Cure

Try all the methods for boredom barking but if you do have to leave him outside for a while, ignore the dog's attention seeking tactics. You could try dropping a few very small titbits out of the window onto the path leading to the door so the dog finds a pleasant reward before he reaches the door and barks. Don't let him see you do this as he will quite likely come and bark under the window to make you drop some more instead of barking at the door!

Guarding the property

Some dogs, particularly the guarding breeds, think it is their job to repel anybody or any animal who dares to come near their garden and that includes the next door neighbour who is trying to clip his hedge, or his children kicking a ball against the fence. Again this is a successful tactic for gaining a quick reaction from the family who rush out to quieten the dog before the neighbour complains yet again.

Cure
Try all the methods outlined above, plus these extra tips.

- It is possible to teach your dog to just sit and point or stare at the 'intruder' without making a sound. Dogs are being successfully trained to do this in drug detection work and I have taught Connie to sit and watch silently as the dustmen and postmen arrive at the bottom of our drive; she is then rewarded by a titbit and attention.
- Another option for a more active dog would be for him to run in to tell you there is someone there and be instantly rewarded, for example, by having his ball thrown.

Frustration
The next door's cat sitting on the fence, smugly taunting the dog from its safe position, can cause a very frustrated type of bark. Children teasing a dog through the fence, or a hedgehog just out of reach beneath the hedge can have the same effect.

Cure
Try the tips suggested above and also offer some distraction, preferably before the dog has become too frustrated.

Time of day
The time of day is quite critical in a lot of cases of problem barking. Some dogs love to go outside at dusk when the scents are exciting and wildlife is on the move. Or perhaps your dog barks when children pass by on their way home from school or when the postman arrives?

Cure
Try to pinpoint these trigger times and make a big effort to keep your dog inside, take him for a walk or even put him in the car at those moments in the day.

223

Excitement

When a dog is let out first thing in the morning he is often very excited and rushes outside barking. He probably knows a fox has visited his garden during the night and thinks if he gets out quickly enough he will catch it this time. A lot of dogs also bark excitedly when they are taken for their walk. If they always bark loudly as they go through the garden it will be an added irritation for the neighbours.

Dominant Dogs

A dominant dog is one that takes on the role of pack leader in the family. He may dominate other dogs, children, the husband or wife, or other members of the household, but still be subservient to one or more people in the home. He may show his dominance towards other dogs in the park, at a local dog club or on his own territory around his house. A dominant dog must not be confused with an aggressive dog, although sometimes a dominant dog will show aggression when his dominance is challenged.

Dominance is not necessarily a permanent condition. For example, a younger dog in the family may challenge the higher-ranking dog to win this higher position. Domestic changes may also change the pack order. For example, a teenager may go away to college and then be challenged by the dog on their return. Dominance can also change hour by hour. A lower-ranking dog, who is lying in a doorway will often not let the higher-ranking one pass although this situation can be reversed later in the day.

Owners often complain that their dog is dominating them if the dog growls at them while he is eating. This is not actually the case. In wild as well as in domestic dogs there is a basic law that says, whoever is in possession of food is entitled to keep it. If a lower-ranking wolf has a bone, even the pack leader will not take it away.

So the question of dominance in dogs is very complex and probably only really understood by dogs and wolves themselves. It is popular to use 'Dominance' as a hook on which to hang many dog problems. If a dog is not behaving in an acceptable way 'experts' will label it as dominant! This is done without thoroughly investigating the problem. Often supposedly dominant dogs are merely confused, anxious or downright terrified!

A really dominant dog may show his superior position in many ways. He may lie at the top of the stairs and dare his owner to come up, or he may leap into bed with his owner and threaten to kill the poor spouse when they try to climb in. Sometimes a dog will sit in front of the television so no one can see and refuse to move, or he will pick the best armchair and growl if challenged. Some dominant dogs are the sweetest natured animals. They have a variety of subtle ways to manipulate and control their subordinate humans. They demand affection whenever they want it and if they don't immediately receive a fuss they will whine and paw at their owners who invariably give in. These dogs demand food, walks and constant access to the garden whenever they want it by whining, barking or scratching at doors. Their long-suffering owners are usually happy to indulge their pets as they are often easygoing people content to let the dog rule the household.

Cure
The aim is to restructure the pack so that the owner becomes the pack leader and his dog is subordinate to him. This does not mean having a cowed or unhappy dog. Re-training the dog for his new position can be achieved through kind methods which he will enjoy.

• Start by doing basic control exercises such as sit, down, come and stay.

225

- Always reward immediately.
- Practise these exercises on neutral territory away from any areas of confrontation.
- Never give an order unless you are positive the dog will carry it out.
- Remove all toys and other possessions and only give them back, one at a time, when he has obeyed an order: for example, sit for a squeaky toy, down for a bone.
- Make sure your dog sits and stays for his dinner.
- Before a walk your dog must sit quietly, if he doesn't, leave him and go away to do something else, then try again.
- Ignore all his demands for attention such as barking or scratching at doors.
- Reward your dog when he sits quietly by your side by stroking and talking to him.
- Bathing, grooming, checking nails and teeth, all help to show who is in charge.
- Only let him through a doorway when he is quiet.
- Areas of confrontation, such as the bedroom (pack leader's den), should be out of bounds.
- Be aware of danger zones such as narrow passages, doorways and confined areas such as small halls.
- Never resort to physical punishment as the dog may retaliate and win!
- Avoid playing 'tug of war' or other rough games where the dog may win.

Dominance Problems Between Dogs
- Generally leave dogs to sort out their own pack order. This is much safer as you might upset the delicate balance between them.
- In certain difficult cases, perhaps when two litter-mates are kept together and are fighting for top position, it might be necessary to interfere.

- It is a good idea to have the slightly lower-ranking dog castrated.
- The higher-ranking dog should be encouraged in his superior position by greeting and feeding him first.
- The dominant dog should have his bed in the best position, preferably nearer the owner's bedroom, he should be first in the car and first out and have the best seat.

By using these methods the pecking order between dogs is more clearly defined. We humans may find this method unfair and would naturally much rather try to elevate the underdog. However, the dogs accept, and are quite happy with the 'pack order' system.

Think Ahead

When deciding whether to have one, or two, puppies from a litter, think very carefully. When young, puppies look so sweet and loving curled up beside one another and it is natural to want to keep two litter-mates together so they have each other for company. However, by the time they reach adolescence trouble can really start, with the puppies sometimes at each other's throats. This is most likely to happen if you have two puppies of the same breed and sex. The worse case often seems to be where two Terrier bitch puppies are kept together – they can be so aggressive towards each other that the only solution is to part with one of them.

Aggression Towards Other Dogs

You probably wonder why your otherwise loving and gentle pet is aggressive towards other dogs. There may be several different reasons for this problem behaviour and understanding them is key to finding a solution.

Territorial
Many dogs guard their house and garden and some dogs even think they own the surrounding area including their familiar local walks. They look on other dogs as intruders and so attack them.

Protective
Some dogs, especially the guarding breeds, think they should protect their owners against anything they view as a threat and this includes other dogs.

Fear
If a dog has been attacked at any time, but especially when still an impressionable puppy, the frightening experience can have a long lasting effect.

Top Dog Syndrome
This kind of dog can attack any dog he thinks may challenge his superior position.

Breed
Certain breeds like Terriers are much more prone to pick a fight than Gun dogs or Hounds that have been bred to live and work in harmony. Try to determine which category your dog falls into and what triggers his aggression. You may find it is a particular breed your dog hates, or just a particular colour or sex.

Cure
- Try to remain relaxed and keep a long, loose lead. Dogs pick up your feelings very easily and know if you are apprehensive or cross. A tight lead confirms this. A dog also feels very trapped and vulnerable on a short, tight lead.

- Avoid narrow paths, gateways and other places where dogs are forced to make eye contact and meet head on. If you see this situation developing, turn around and walk in the same direction as the strange dog until there is enough space between you, for you to turn around and continue your walk.
- Improve your basic control of your dog. Practise simple obedience exercises in the house, the garden and especially on walks to help build up your control when meeting other dogs. Play control games, such as sitting for the ball.
- Distraction always helps. Use food or toys as pleasurable distractions. In more severe cases the dog's daily ration of food can be split up into small portions and used as rewards for good behaviour when meeting other dogs. At first walk as far away as possible from other dogs but keep within sight of them. Reward your dog for his good behaviour with one portion of food and also praise lavishly. Continue doing this, gradually reducing the distance between you and the other dog, rewarding your dog each time. Try not to rush this exercise. Not only will the food act as a very welcome distraction because your dog will be hungry but he will also start to associate something pleasant with other dogs.

Other More Drastic Methods

- If there is a real danger of your dog biting another dog consider a muzzle. If one is used make it really pleasurable for him, as it should not be a punishment. Get one that you can still feed titbits through. Sometimes because the owner becomes so much more relaxed, the dog gives up his aggressive ways and the muzzle can then be removed.
- Castration can sometimes work depending on the cause but it isn't an instant cure for all aggression problems.

229

Treatment in Specific Cases

Territorial Problems
Try to walk your dog in lots of different areas. He may be less aggressive if he is taken by car to a new place.

Protective Dogs
Talk to the owners of the other dog while relaxing and feeding your own dog. If he thinks you are quite happy to have other people and their dogs nearby he is more likely to follow your example.

Fearful Dogs
Fearful dogs need their confidence building up gradually. Try to introduce them to gentle, quiet, good-tempered dogs where there is plenty of space so they do not feel crowded or intimidated.

Top Dog
This kind of dog is often quite dominant. Do lots of work to reduce his dominance so he knows his place in the family pack. See pages 224–7 for specific tips on reducing dominance.

Difficult Breeds
Sadly this just makes your task a little harder but good basic training does work!

Lastly, remember to praise good behaviour, ignore bad behaviour whenever practicable, and never use aggression yourself.

Separation Anxiety

This area of behavioural problems happens with dogs that just cannot cope with being left on their own and become very distressed when separated from their owners. This condition is often seen in rescued dogs that are insecure and when placed in a new home are so desperate not to lose their new owner they will not let them out of sight and anxiously follow them from room to room.

Common Triggers

- Domestic stress or a change within the household can trigger the problem. Altering either the dog's usual routine or the owner's can be enough to cause anxiety and stress to some dogs. Many dogs adapt well to being left alone for quite long periods while their owners are at work if they have always known this regular routine, but if the pattern is interrupted for a while it can then be difficult for some dogs to cope when they are left alone again. Obviously the problem is exacerbated if the owners are feeling stressed, depressed or unwell at home and the dog simply cannot understand this change.
- Moving house can also provoke separation anxiety, with settled dogs feeling very worried. It's worth remembering that it is not only during the day that dogs cannot cope with being alone, they often feel vulnerable and isolated

231

when they are put in a strange room, especially if it is some distance from your bedroom.

- Dogs that are used to open-plan houses where they have access to all rooms can feel unable to cope alone if circumstances change. Again some breeds are more prone to this condition than others: for instance, active Collies who instinctively jump up and follow their human sheep as soon as they move, and one-man dogs such as German Shepherds that form a strong attachmant to just one person.
- Thunderstorms, fireworks or other loud noises can trigger this condition in a previously relaxed dog.
- When two dogs have always been kept together and rely on one another for company, if one dies, the remaining dog often cannot cope alone.

Signs of anxiety

- Dogs may become very agitated and distressed whenever their owners try to leave.
- They may occasionally become aggressive, start growling and even biting.

Symptoms of anxiety often begin shortly after the dog is left. Many owners complain that their dog has wrecked the house after being left for just ten minutes. Neighbours sometimes report howling or barking as the owners' car drives away.

When the dog is left alone, one or more of the following may occur:

- Destructiveness, including shredding of wallpaper and even plaster.
- Attacking doors, door handles and frames, which can

232

sometimes be badly chewed, and biting and scratching any floor coverings in front of the door.

- Ripping curtains, probably as the dog is trying to look through or get out of the window.
- Armchairs and sofas, particularly where the dog's favourite person sits, are often a target – the familiar smell is comforting so the dog will scratch, bite and burrow into it.
- Wetting and defecation are common.
- Barking, whining, howling, pacing, panting and even self-mutilation are also seen.

Cure

Gradually desensitise your dog to being left on his own. Start by leaving him in a familiar room where you have scattered small, tasty titbits over the floor which will take him a little while to find and eat. This will happily occupy and distract your dog as you leave the room. Casually tell him to, 'Mind the house' as you go. At this early stage it is helpful to sing or talk to yourself as you leave, so that your dog will be reassured by your voice and know you are not far away. At this point it is vital that you only leave the dog for a few minutes. You should aim to return before he has eaten all the treats and is still relaxed and quiet. On no account leave him until he becomes worried. Your leaving and returning should be very relaxed and casual – remember just how sensitive dogs are to our moods and how they copy them. This treatment should be continued, gradually lengthening the time you leave your dog alone.

The next step is to split up the leaving process into small segments. If your normal routine is to put on your coat, pick up your car keys, lock up the house and then drive away, you should just do the first action before returning

233

to your dog. Continue until you can put all the parts together. It's really important not to rush any of these stages because if your dog becomes distressed you will have undone all your good work and you will have to start from the beginning again.

When the dog is relaxed and confident enough to be left for a short time, the following tips will help him settle:

- Make sure he has been exercised and has performed his toilet.
- Try to leave him at a time when he is usually sleepy.
- Leave him in a warm, familiar room to encourage him to feel sleepy.
- Give him one of your old sweaters to cuddle up to. Sleep with it the night before so it smells comfortingly of you.
- Buy a hollow bone and stuff it with goodies such as brown bread and dripping and small dog treats. Arrange them so that some are easy to reach while others need work. This will provide interest and help keep him occupied.
- A new chew toy also helps, as chewing reduces stress.
- Try to find educational toys to occupy your dog while you are out.
- Remember that dogs, like children, are far more interested in new toys or ones they haven't played with for a while, so try to provide something different when you leave.
- It goes without saying that if your dog does do something wrong while you are away, do not punish him as this will only intensify his anxiety complex. If the damage is already done the dog will also not understand why he is being punished.

Helpful Tips

- If you normally have the radio on when you are at home, try leaving it on when you go out.
- Leave by the back door instead of the front, or vice versa.
- Try parking your car away from the house as it is sometimes the sound of the car leaving which triggers dogs' anxiety.
- Make frequent short trips outside to the dustbin, shed, clothesline etc, leaving your dog indoors.
- Try feeding your dog his dinner then leaving him alone in the kitchen so he has pleasant associations of being left. In the early stages, return to the kitchen before he has finished.
- Aim to have a dog that loves company both in and out of the house but is also laid back about being on his own.
- If you are off work for some time, try to keep to a similar routine as far as possible.
- A substitute den – for instance a dog cage covered with a blanket – can help some dogs, especially ones that are fearful of loud noises such as thunder. Make sure your dog views his den as a safe haven, never somewhere he is sent as punishment. It should be warm and comfortable and the door should be left open.
- If you are moving house, try to place your dog's bed near to the heart of the house or close to the main bedroom. He would probably choose to actually sleep in your bedroom but if you don't want that, use a baby gate across the door with your dog's bed on the other side. This should ensure he doesn't feel isolated. Reassure him while he is still quiet and don't wait until he cries before speaking to him.
- If you have more than one dog, make sure they still

have plenty of interaction with their human pack as well as each other. Treat the dogs as individuals and separate them on occasion for games, walks and car rides. This will all help a dog cope if one of the others later dies.

- Start training a new puppy or older new arrival to be happy and relaxed when alone from day one. The longer you leave it the harder it will be!

Introducing a New Pet

$\mathbf{B}$ ringing home a new puppy, older dog or introducing a cat to live with the resident dog, or a new dog to a resident cat, can be a traumatic experience. Forward planning is essential if you want introductions to run smoothly.

Exchange of Scents

This is particularly useful when introducing a cat.

- Before you bring home the new pet, try to arrange to swap over a piece of bedding so the new pet can smell the resident's scent and vice versa.
- Keep the new pet separate from the family dog for a few days if possible while more scent is exchanged. It is far easier and less traumatic for animals to gradually get to know about each other through this exchange of scent.
- Use a time-share system for different rooms where each animal has access to the same places but crucially at different times.
- Swap toys, feeding bowls and bedding between the pets but never let a young puppy rip up your dog's favourite toy or bedding.
- Make sure that all family members and visitors understand that at this stage the animals are being supervised and remember to shut all doors.

Supervised Meetings

- The next stage is to introduce the animals to each other in a pleasurable and controlled way.
- The use of a pen can be helpful for a new cat because one animal can be put in a safe pen while the other is loose in the room.
- A dog could also be kept on a lead.
- Very gradually reduce the distance between the animals so they remain calm and unstressed.

Distractions

- While the early introductions are taking place use pleasant distractions.
- Food is an excellent distraction – use very small pieces of food such as cheese for dogs or some cream-cheese or butter for cats.
- Choose foods that take some time to eat but which are a special tasty treat.
- Make sure both animals are looking away from each other as you feed them.
- The next stage is to use laps and leads, so you will need two people for this – again use food but also introduce toys as a distraction.
- With dogs and cats together, roll balls away from the cat, not towards it.
- The idea of these distractions is to build up the association that being together means food, fuss and play.
- Always praise good, calm behaviour.
- If a dog gets too excited, quietly put him out of the room for just a minute, then begin again keeping him at a greater distance.

Escape Routes

When introductions between a cat and dog are more advanced and the pets are loose together make quite sure the cat has safe escape routes through the house – to the cat flap, litter tray, or to food bowls. There should also be high safe refuges such as windowsills so that the cat cannot be cornered.

- Baby gates can work well to restrict small dogs, while allowing cats access.
- It is also important for the older dog to have a special quiet retreat away from the bouncy new puppy.

Maintaining Routines

It is important for the resident pet to keep to its usual routines. It is hard enough for him to accept a newcomer without also missing out on familiar walks, meal times and play.

Remember: never leave recently introduced pets alone unsupervised until you are absolutely certain they will be safe together.

Problems with Two Dogs

The idea of two dogs companionably living together is very appealing and many people with more than one dog are extremely happy together. However, the situation can bring a whole range of problems. People often mistakenly think that having a second dog will cure a behaviour problem with their first. They may assume that two puppies will keep each other company and make their own amusements; and they will, although you won't necessarily like the results! The temptation is to treat the dogs as a pair rather than two individuals which can lead to the dogs not responding to their owners and being very hard to control either in the house, garden or out on walks.

Optimistic owners assume the second dog will conveniently pick up and learn all the good points from the first dog but none of the bad. They may overlook the fact that a pair of dogs is much more likely to run off on walks, go hunting, or even escape from the garden and go sheep worrying. If one dog is aggressive to other dogs on walks, its companion will often join in.

When two dogs sleep together, eat together and walk together all the time, they then find it very difficult if they eventually have to cope on their own if the other dies. The remaining one can suffer from depression, insecurity or loss of appetite.

Sometimes the problem is one of aggression and this can

arise even between family dogs that previously got along with one another. If the aggression is extreme and cannot be resolved one of them may even have to be re-homed.

Preventing Aggression

- Choose dogs of different sexes, ages and breeds. Dogs are pack animals who both need and understand the structure of the family pack, including both humans and dogs. If for instance you have two litter sisters of Jack Russell puppies, they may be fine until they reach puberty at which point they can have terrible fights to resolve who is top dog. With our children we always try to be completely fair and treat them as equals but this simply does not work with dogs.
- Some breeds are more laid back and tolerant than others. Dogs that have been bred to work together like Gun dogs, or Hounds are more likely to get on than, say, Terriers.
- A dog and a bitch usually get on well together.
- A very large dog often seems to think a tiny dog is a puppy and treats it as such, whilst the tiny dog thinks it is a big dog and often dominates its larger friend and becomes top dog. This sounds odd but can work quite well!
- Decide which dog is top dog and make sure this one has everything first, while the lower-ranking one must wait his turn. Food, fuss, greetings, being let out into the garden, put into the car – the top dog must always have these things first.
- The top dog must have the best positions in the house, the best dog bed which is closer to his owner's bedroom or in it, if that is allowed.
- Elevated places such as the top of the stairs are a privilege for the top dog. Similarly, he should have the best position in the car.

- It should however be made very clear to this dog that he may be top dog but he is certainly not top of the human pack.
- Adding a third dog to an established two-dog pack can easily cause disharmony.

Sometimes dogs that have previously got along well together suddenly become very aggressive towards each other. Often this is because something has upset the structure of the pack; this might be something apparently insignificant, at least to a human. In one case I treated, a visitor looking after the dogs while the owners were on holiday fed the underdog first, which was enough to trigger aggression in the top dog.

Illness, hospitalisation or operations after which one of the dogs receives extra fuss and attention can all have an effect on dog relationships. When a dog returns home from an operation and a stay at the vet he smells strange and may look different: perhaps he's wobbly on his legs or is wearing a large stand-up collar around his neck. All these things could be worrying for his companion.

A change of place can trigger problems. I know of cases where the family dogs always got on well until they were put in kennels together. Moving house or changing where they sleep can all cause stress for dogs.

Cure
- If relationships are deteriorating reinforce the pack order and make sure you are clear about which is top dog.
- Watch for situations that may provoke a fight. Remove prized possessions such as bones, toys and treats – even a dropped crumb from the table can start the trouble.
- Be particularly careful when greeting the dogs.

- Beware of competitive situations, such as both dogs racing to meet someone.
- Watch for the first signs of tension such as the dogs staring at each other and distract them quickly.
- Certain places can trigger aggression: such as doorways, gateways, narrow halls and stairways. Be aware of this and be ready to distract one of the dogs so they can pass one another without losing face.
- Use baby gates to separate the dogs or shut them in different rooms if you are going out or cannot supervise them carefully.
- Sometimes wearing muzzles while they are in the same room can help but do not leave them alone with them on.
- If the aggression has been caused by a change in routine reinstate this as soon as possible.
- Hormones or medical conditions can cause aggression so do check with your vet. A bitch coming into season or having a false pregnancy may be bad tempered.
- I have known of entire dogs that get on well together and castrated dogs that fight, but with dogs of the same sex it sometimes works to have one dog neutered and one not, helping to make it clear to the dogs who has the highter position in the pack.
- It is possible to simulate neutering with veterinary treatment to see if this works. Your vet can advise you.

In many cases harmony can be successfully restored and the dogs will live happily together. I had a two-dog family for many years, which worked extremely well.

Seasonal Tips

Christmas

Christmas is an exciting, busy time but the extra visitors, bustle and atmosphere can be very unsettling for dogs who just don't understand what's going on. A few simple precautions can help keep everyone, including your dog, happy and relaxed.

- Keep to your pet's normal routine of feeding, walking and bed times as far as possible. This will help to keep them contented and stress free during the excitement of the festivities.
- Feed dogs their normal diet. It is tempting to give lots of rich goodies so they can enjoy Christmas too, but you may not enjoy Boxing Day cleaning up the results of upset tummies! Just add a few tiny tasty morsels to their food.
- Stick to your usual house rules. If your dog does not normally sleep on the bed or sofa, do not allow him to do so as a special Christmas treat. He could be very confused and not want to revert to normal afterwards.
- Conversely if your dog always has the entire sofa to lounge on, he will be less than happy if he has to share it with house guests.
- The same rule applies to feeding titbits at the table – if

your family do not do it, tactfully tell your guests not to.

- Do not forget regular toilet trips, especially for young or old dogs.
- Provide a quiet retreat where your cat or dog can rest in peace.
- With lots of people coming and going be extra careful that doors and gates are not left open for a dog to get out.
- Even a well-trained dog might seize the opportunity to steal the turkey or Christmas cake if they are temptingly left out in the kitchen while everybody is busy partying at the other end of the house. To avoid temptation, check that everything is put away.
- Keep an eye on your rubbish bins. Make sure they are not overflowing and have their lids fully closed, especially if they have turkey bones in them. The bones are dangerous and when a dog has had the reward of raiding the rubbish bin just once, he will carry on doing it.
- The Christmas tree is a temptation for the inquisitive pet. Make sure the tree is secure with no fragile or dangerous decorations within reach and avoid leaving your dog unsupervised in the same room.
- The presents beneath the tree are another target to rip open and investigate.
- Remember that normal chocolates are dangerous for dogs. Only give them dog chocs.
- Jealousy between two dogs can escalate with the excitement of receiving presents, or even watching their human family opening their presents. This can result in a fight. Separate the dogs while they open their presents if you think this might happen.

Fireworks and Thunder

Many dogs are frightened by loud noises, whether sudden claps of thunder or firework displays. If you are training a new puppy, gradually expose him to a wide variety of sounds. If you can, start a long way from the source of the noise and slowly decrease the distance, making sure your puppy is confident and relaxed. It helps if the people and other animals with the puppy are also calm and confident because your puppy will copy the behaviour of his pack. If any companions are fearful, your puppy will also be afraid.

Helpful Hints

- Make audio or video recordings of thunder storms, fireworks and explosions and play these gradually – perhaps while your dog is eating so he will have pleasant associations with these sights and sounds. Although dogs seem to know these are not the real thing, they are still helpful when the real thing is going on outside.
- It is vital that your dog is relaxed throughout, so don't be tempted to rush.
- Do not sympathise with your dog as he will just assume that you are frightened too. Instead, try to appear bright and confident.
- Reward your dog's calm, relaxed behaviour.
- Try to distract him with a noisy, exciting game.
- Some people find a car ride works if that's practical.
- Try throwing a tasty titbit immediately, each time there is a loud noise.
- Begin these distraction tactics before your dog shows he is afraid. Once a dog is really fearful he will not respond.
- If you know there are going to be noisy fireworks and

you are thinking of using sedatives, talk to your vet well in advance.

- Some dogs like to creep away to a safe dark refuge when frightened, so provide a warm, dark den – you could try a blanket draped over a low table or cage, or access to the bedroom where they can hide under a bed.
- Before a firework display, or as soon as you hear distant thunder, draw the curtains and play your tapes or videos of thunder or fireworks quite loudly, although only when your dog is completely relaxed while they are playing.
- You could also try playing music in different rooms, especially in unusual places or with different music playing in each room. It sounds dreadful but it worked with one of my dogs.
- Keep pets indoors on bonfire night and take extra care that doors and gates are shut as some dogs can panic and run off.